UNDERSTANDING A MAN

EMPOWERING WOMEN WITH TOOLS FOR LASTING RELATIONSHIPS

Elam B. King

Printed in the United States of America
ISBN 13: 9780578192703
ISBN: 0578192705
Library of Congress Control Number: 2017916567
KS Media and Publishing, Chesapeake, VA

www.understandingaman.com

Table of Contents

Dedication

To Adrienne E. Bell and the Wifeability movement helping to inspire and educate women to be the wives that GOD has called them to be. Keep impacting lives, sharing your vision, and teaching the principles of a successful relationship.

To the friends and family that helped me through my challenges. I want you to know that you kept me motivated to push forward despite all odds and to know me, is to know you have blessed someone along your journey.

To my wife and children, you are my "why" and I look forward to continuing to share the rest of my life with you. Thank you for your sacrifice of time. Thank you for believing in me.

Acknowledgements

I WOULD LIKE to take a moment and acknowledge the sources for this inspiration. God being first to give me the vision to be a vessel in His Kingdom. Michelle King for providing ongoing guidance, love, and support. My loving parents for making the first sacrifices for my life and for being my benchmark. My two older brothers Aldolphus and Shaheen King for watching out for me when we were growing up. My younger brothers Anthony Dicosmo and Zachary King for being my sounding boards over the years. Spiritual mentor and friend Adrienne Bell. Bishop, cousin, and friend Chancey King and his wife Cycloria King. My church family and friends of Greater Works Tabernacle in Conley, GA.

Business mentors Donna Bingham and Lanier Price. Business partners and personal development family: Kerens Jean Baptiste, Janson Cross, Doremus Diggs, Zenja Dunn, Keith Fatherly, John Fleming, Michael Fowles, Jareed Hall, Geoffrey Hudson, Cheryl McKay, and Jamal Williams. Over the past 20 years, at some point you said something or gave guidance to me that was life changing. Thank you for the personal development manuals and keeping me focused.

The people that have touched me at some point through your words of encouragement and leading by example: Lashada Allen, Lorenzo Aytes, Nyema Barnes Vincent Kelly Bennett, Chris Brown, Tony Foster, Paras Griffin, James Hawkins, Stephanie Hill, Antonio Martez, Marshall Mitchell, Joi Pearson, Robert Price, Spencer Moore, Joey Reasor, Eugene Thomas, Stacy Reviere, Alan and Crystal Watterson, Selvin and Glennetta White, and the late Napolean Meadors.

The men that I surveyed, interviewed, and gathered data from. The progressive men that inspire me in some way and whom I have the utmost respect for: Raasan Austin, Trey Barnette, Donald Bell, Porter Bingham, Harold "Poncho"

Brinkley, Charles Butler, Barry Case, Brian E. Clarke, Rosbyn Shon Elliott, Omar Finley, James Foulke, John Telley Gilliard, Kevin Gray, Ryan C. Greene, Chris Jackson, Bishop Chancey King, Zachary King, Rodney Lawson, Delante Murphy, Rafiq Shakur, Rod Shipman, and Samuel Lee Smith III.

To all - thank you for your time and efforts in helping to put this project together. I love each of you and look forward to the many successes that God is unfolding in your lives.

Our humanity's progress is heavily dependent on how many of its members begin to dive deeper into a state of seeking to understand versus the ever so popular alternative position...only wanting to be understood. This lack of understanding when it comes to the challenges within marriages and relationships has caused so many women and men to simply put up with criticism, defensiveness, and contempt and using those past experiences to negatively adjust their future expectations.

Those expectations lead to decisions which in turn will have a generational impact. Unhappiness, settling, disloyalty, struggle, and the list of other adjectives that are feared in the quest for a suitable partner are only reflections of the strategies used in the past.

Often, we make up guidelines as we go and risk getting attached to people who could have been completely avoided while missing out on building that unbreakable foundation with a true life-partner. As the emotions flare up, those ever so important questions that needed to be asked are pushed to the back burner. As they adjust to each other's rhythm, the expectation volume gently gets lowered.

Once the volume can no longer be silenced, the cycle repeats itself, however, a piece of infinitely valued essence has been given to someone who did not deserve it. Yes, strength was gained in the process but that does not change the time and energy put into another life lesson.

Today is an entirely new beginning.

Understanding A Man: Empowering Women With Tools For Lasting Relationships takes its reader through doors that often remain closed. It is designed to open the lines of communication prior to the beginning of the relationship and adds to existing relationships because when more insight is layered into a solid foundation, the new dynamics create an even stronger bond.

Elam King, a happily married man of 14 years with 6 beautiful children peels back all of the layers of growth that he and his wife encountered along their journey. He also personally interviews 24 men from various backgrounds who were specifically selected due to the life they've led. Marriage, child-rearing, spirituality, and relationships are just a few of the many topics that are covered.

The value of any interview is not determined because of the answers to the questions. The true quality of the questions is what makes such a huge difference, so Elam's experience and track record in regards to his marriage add an invaluable dimension to the reader.

My life would not be the same if it were not for the example that was set by Elam when I first entered the corporate world in 2001. The personal and business development tools that he helped to build a life for myself that far exceeded what I could have imagined at the time, so I am truly thankful to have reaped the benefits of the words in this book.

Get ready because in the upcoming pages you have will have another tool at your disposal. Remember, the benefit that is received from any tool always comes down to how well the person understands how to use it.

Let the building begin……

Kinja Dixon

Re-Creation Strategist

"Human nature" is one of those phrases that often gets thrown around, but one that most can't precisely define. Our thoughts, feelings, and behaviors are shaped by both our individual experiences and the environment in which we are exposed to throughout our upbringing. As you look at what some consider "human nature", it's easy to see that cultural differences can explain some of the differences in the way we look at relationships, but certainly not all. What we do know is human nature has us begging for relationships that meet our most basic and intimate needs in a variety of ways: sexual, emotional, intellectual, or physical. ***Understanding A Man*** is a brilliant and riveting gem where Elam King has served us a silver platter of everything we ever wanted to know about how to truly reach an emotional peak with the kind of man you would want to bring home to meet your family. The ground-breaking information he has shared here comes straight from the men who are begging women to be the "woman of their dreams", and they are telling us exactly what they are looking for, but so unable to find.

Let's face it, a few women are going to read this title and become emotionally charged before ever getting to the first chapter. Sexual rejection, a hot topic in any relationship, was discussed in such a compelling way that I walked away with a whole new perspective on why saying "honey, I'm too tired" is so detrimental to a relationship. How do men really see this? As women, we sometimes think that men place too much importance on the act itself, and therefore we feel we can use it as leverage. Far too many women don't see or acknowledge the significant pain, isolation, and confusion men feel when the woman they have chosen to be their wife rejects their need for sex. ***Understanding A Man*** is a priceless guide to how men perceive this rejection and their need for a deeper connection to the one they choose to be their wife. In Chapter 8, he shares the invaluable, honest opinions of the 24 different men he interviewed, offering all the ladies out there an in-depth view of what is in the mind of the man of their dreams. Do men want sex as a form of control or are men deeply and physically hurt by a lack of sex with their wives? Grab the book and find out.

As a fellow author, to say I was honored to be a part of the foreword for ***Understanding A Man***, is an understatement. I have known Elam King for many years and have long admired how he has truly redefined who he is as a man, stood true to his moral compass, and has shown his family what it means to love unconditionally. He has gained the respect of many men and women alike for holding true to his values and seeking to restore the traditional sense of connection a husband and wife were meant to have in the eyes of God. As a wife of 21 years, I recently set out on a path to discover a deeper understanding of what it takes to achieve the kind of human connection that is truly unbreakable, the kind of biblical proportions. This journey has highlighted the need our society has for each of us to muster the necessary courage needed to examine, confront, and embrace the role we play within our own personal relationship. ***Understanding A Man***, offers an unparalleled opportunity to empower ourselves as women by learning what real men (the kind you would want walking through life with your daughter) are begging for. The tools suggested throughout offer us the chance to truly define our personal relationships by aligning what the "good guys" are telling us they want with the roles that God created for each of us. As they say, knowledge is power. Get ready to build a thriving relationship as you gain an understanding of spiritual connection that you have never known.

Crystal Watterson
Best Selling Author and Relationship Coach

Picture yourself walking in a room. Standing around you, are twenty-four big brothers who care for you....They talk. You listen.

Introduction

WHAT IF THERE was a manual that looked into the topics that men want women to understand about the way we think? What if there was a manual that helped empower women with the tools that allow them to navigate through certain pitfalls they encounter in romantic relationships? What if there was a manual that helped women understand the way strong, progressive, positive, and intellectually developed men think?

For far too long, women have been seeking advice from the wrong sources. For example, I have encountered many times when a woman is having a problem in her relationship, she will pick up the phone and call her female friend. Unfortunately, this same friend is probably single and still trying to navigate her way through her own relationship. We have a tendency as people to seek knowledge from someone who is at the same level, if not below our level, but then expect to find a solution and rise to whatever challenge is in front of us. Conversely, in school, if you are having a problem in math class, you go to the teacher, get some extra help, or hire a tutor. If you want to learn how to play an instrument, you go to an instructor. If you're an athlete, and you want to become better, you go to the coach. I could give you countless scenarios of how we are hardwired to seek guidance by going to the right source for answers on how to elevate ourselves in many different areas, but when it comes to our relationships, we often seek the wrong sources.

The purpose of this manual is to:

1. Provide a comprehensive understanding of how men think in romantic relationships to women *who have* had a father figure throughout their lifetime.

2. Provide a comprehensive understanding of how men think in romantic relationships to women *who have not* had a father figure in their lives. Often times women have not had the chance to watch and listen to a man as they were growing up, which causes them to miss the opportunity to understand how men think on various topics. This can cause a psychological setback and misunderstanding of their significant other that many times they do not see until later in life. This manual will give an opportunity for women to understand the way men think and may help prevent the pitfalls women run into with their relationships, particularly in marriage.
3. Help men validate their thoughts and provide direction for their ongoing journey. Men do not express themselves very often as we are generally not taught to do so as we are maturing into manhood. Our thoughts can seem isolated and confusing if we do not have others that we can speak with and express how we think and feel in our relationships. This manual will serve as a benchmark and allow men to feel more comfortable in knowing that there are many other men in our society who mirror some of the same thought patterns.

I had the honor of interviewing twenty-four men about various topics that are important in dating, marriage, sex, and spirituality. These men are the type of men that you would want your daughter to bring home to you for the Holidays.

Picture yourself walking into a room. Standing around you, are twenty-four big brothers who care for you. Each of them will share with you their feelings on topics that you need to know. Although there may be more topics or challenges that you are facing, the topics discussed are ones they feel you should understand about men. They talk. You listen.

At the end of each chapter, there are some empowerment tools that you need to implement inside of your respective relationships. These will be the tools to remember and will assist you with cultivating a lasting relationship.

Your high standards should be congruent with a high level of understanding your man.

Chapter 1

High Standards: Stop the Madness!

Ladies, I would like you to take a moment and think about how you expect nothing less than the best for yourself. I think it's great to have high standards. Men should treat you right. Make you feel special. "Treat you like a queen" as the saying goes.

Is that a bad thing? **Nope.**

The question I presented to the men for this chapter was, "**How do you feel when you hear a woman has high standards and how can a woman have high standards without having a checklist?'**

Trey Barnette: *"I think that a lot of accomplished women have unrealistic high standards and what I tend to find out is that these* ***checklists*** *contradict themselves.. A woman who wants a man* ***who is*** *ambitious and a man that's forever growing and accomplishes things, but they also want this man that can give them all his time, be around twenty-four seven and not have any other things or distractions... That just doesn't match because as you know any man that's ambitious, any man that's about his business, he has to sacrifice time just to be able to do those things... and that's probably the major contradictory quality of men that I see on the checklist from women because whenever I have conversation with women, and I bring that up, they kind of have this stunned look as if they got stung by a bee...and you look at them and you say, you can't expect me to make all this money but then* ***at the same time have all of this time....*** *what I find in women is that there is an unrealistic checklist and that's why you find a lot of accomplished females that are out here and that are still single, looking for this man that is unrealistic."*

But let's go deeper.

We are **PRACTICING** being a man every day. You have been comfortable with other people your entire life practicing their craft. As a matter of fact, you even paid some of them. Think about it. A doctor is practicing medicine, yet, you allow him to operate on you. ALL doctors are practicing medicine and sometimes they get it right, and other times they may get it wrong. Maybe you know of someone who was prescribed the wrong medication... Did that stop you from going to the doctor? Why is it so difficult for women to ease up on the checklist for a man concerning romantic relationships? Do you expect him to get it all right the first time? Is that really fair? Do you get it right the first time?

To the ladies with the **ridiculous** check marks that a man needs to have, you too may be missing that mark.

Ryan Greene: *For example, they want a man to be over six feet tall... well only 17% of men in the world are over 6 feet tall and that's real statistics. So you've already limited your pool. We have women who are 5'2 talking about being with a man over six feet tall... well no, you don't need, that. You're only 5'2 so you can deal with a man whose 5'6 or 5'5 and you good... I think those are some of the things that are unrealistic. I was having a conversation with a woman the other day who said that the man has to make six figures. Can you imagine a woman back in the 1960s and 1970s saying they need to have a man that makes six figures? How silly does that sound?... because women are trying to live up to the standards that we see on TV... back in the day women looked for men with quality and you weren't stuck with the superficial things that you can brag to your friends about...that's what a lot of this stuff is... Women just want to be able to brag to their friends and then you'll have women say, "it doesn't matter what he does for a job", but then when I go and introduce them to someone who drives a forklift, then they think "I can't brag about him to my girls"(in their head) and not realize the guy out there on the forklift is making six figures too but because he walks outside to work with Timberland boots, then he's not looking sexy enough to brag about... let's talk about the man who's running a restaurant. They make $60,000 to $70,000 a year as a General Manager but a lot of women are going to say I don't want a restaurant manager because he works at a restaurant ... they're not looking at what he can do and what he can be and that's where I'm talking about realistic expectations. You can have high standards and you should. I understand you are a woman out there dating and yes, you are a catch for a man and you are a jewel and you should have high standards, but let's make sure that your high standards are on the moral grounds of a man who* *loves you, a man who cares for you, a man who is loyal, willing to take care of you and not that superficial stuff... because he can have six figures today and tomorrow he'll be unemployed... are you still going to love him?*

Ladies, if you are struggling with your standards and trying to figure out if you are missing the mark, I want to give you the best advice to fix this: Whatever you have on your list, needs to be at the same level you are at. The lady that makes a certain high-level income, can understand the man who also makes that type of income. She can understand the sacrifices of time and/or money he has to make in order to reach those levels. So if you want your future husband to be great, be at that same level of greatness. Along the way, you will develop the wisdom to handle the type of man you're asking for.

Do you want a man who can provide financial security for your household? Well it takes way more than love to pay the bills in a home. I am not giving him an excuse to always lean on to neglect you and/or your family. I am simply sharing with you that the level of financial security you may want from your man has a cost that you need to be willing to understand. Your High Standards should be congruent with a high level of understanding your man.

For those of you who are saying you want him to have certain characteristics or certain qualities, let me encourage you to **GO WORK ON YOURSELF**. What type of personal development are you engaging in? Are you reading any personal improvement books to help develop your character? What negative characteristics about yourself are you shedding? If you have not been able to maintain a steady relationship, yet you have these high standards that you want a man to have, you may be fooling yourself. You may be holding onto negative qualities that could bring the relationship down, but you want him to be on point from day one? That's madness. Go to work on yourself as hard as you can. As you do that, you will build a better appreciation and understanding of how a man travels his journey and **practices** being a man. And here is a secret: if he sees you working on yourself to become better, it will encourage him to continue to do the same.

I think a great rule of thumb for a checklist is practicing **The 80-20 Rule.**

Raasan Austin: *I would utilize the 80-20 rule if he has 80% of what you need, the other 20% you're just going to have to adjust and learn to get along without it and as long as the 20%*

is not an immediate deal-breaker, you'll be fine... so 80%: for example he has a good job and treats you nice, is loyal, etc.... and then the other 20%: maybe he leaves the seat up on the toilet, or maybe he has a favorite pair of pants that are too tight to your liking.... you have to learn to work with it if the 80% is there, then maybe you need to think about grabbing that guy up.

I think the best part about this rule is that it gives you room to adjust. It also gives you the ability to grow. What may have been a deal-breaker when you were 20, is not always the same when you are 30 or 40. Be open to adjusting your standards and not so stuck on him having to meet every point on your list.

Be the change you want in your life.

Empowerment Tools:

- Always remember, a man is **PRACTICING** being a man.
- If you want a great man, **go be a great woman.**
- Use **The 80/20 Rule** for your revised checklist
- Choose your 80% and choose it wisely.

...when a woman maximizes her role in the home, she becomes more powerful than the man.

CHAPTER 2

Ms. Independent or Interdependent?

I BELIEVE A man loves having a hard-working, progressive woman by his side. Some feel being in a relationship with a woman of that stature can come with conditions of being more "mouthy" and having more feelings of entitlement. The question I presented to the men for this chapter was, **"How does dating or being married to an independent woman make you feel?"** This chapter may step on a few toes so let me take a moment to encourage you that if you feel some kind of way about it, then humbly I ask that you table your emotions and do some deeper soul-searching. When you complete this chapter, you will understand how we feel about certain attributes of the **Independent Woman.**

Let me start by saying that some ladies have been set up for failure in this area. I'm sorry. I didn't do it. Years ago when women came into the workforce, they ran into what has culturally been called "a man's world." Not only was it difficult for women to obtain a job in what was considered a conservative society, but it was also difficult for women to climb the "corporate ladder." Female members of Generation X and Y saw this injustice happening to the Baby Boomer and decided to focus on empowering themselves as well as increase their educational development in order to successfully compete in the workforce. What was the end result? The female population, particularly women of color, are the most educated demographic in America. This aggressive movement of intellectual achievement and social empowerment has resulted in supervisory roles, upper management positions, constant promotion, and an Executive seat at the conference room table. Being the Father of 4 fearless daughters, I can appreciate this great accomplishment.

For some women, in her plight to gain acceptance at the conference table, she may have lost her influence at the kitchen table. **WAIT**...do not leave...just hear me out. When I say kitchen table I **DO NOT** mean that in a derogatory or disrespectful manner. I mean that she may have lost the skill it takes to successfully maintain her home.

Let's take a woman who is married, has one or two kids, and maybe she's a Director or Vice President at a company. She works all day hiring and firing as well as making decisions without needing permission. She has complete autonomy in her office and well respected among her peers. Whether she is a doctor, lawyer, or maybe she just works a regular 9-5pm job but she is educated, progressive and quite verbal in her business dealings throughout the day. At the end of her work day, she arrives home and crosses the threshold of her home, she has to transform into a *submissive* wife and an *attentive* mother. Society has been coaching her throughout her lifetime how important it is to be a mother, so she easily slips into that role when she comes home. But as far as being a submissive wife, this role often becomes an option and becomes difficult to transition into.

So here comes the man, the CEO of the home, perhaps asking her a question or making a decision and instead of the woman following his leadership, she rejects her role and in walks **emasculation.** Here comes the aggressive woman that she has to be in the workforce telling him what she refuses to do in the home. Keep in mind most of the time if you are a successful woman in the workforce, you are probably married or are dating a strong man, which means he's not used to anyone talking down to him, particularly his mate. Do you think you can rip your man's **proverbial balls** off with your verbal assaults along with your aggressive mannerisms, and expect him to still want to continuously come home to you at night or be in a relationship with you? The answer is, no. You could have the best sex and the best head game he can stand and you will still experience some relationship challenges if your verbal communication emasculates your husband.

When a man hears the word "independent woman" he is thinking one of two things. On one hand, he's happy with being with a woman who can take care of herself. He is also thinking about the strategic collaboration he can have with her long-term. But on the other hand, he's thinking **"how much of this**

aggressive nature that can come with an independent woman can I deal with?"

Unfortunately, some men will become strategic in the relationship in order to ensure his emotional needs are being met while his home remains in one piece. He will resolve that his woman will be a good mother and financial contributor to the home but in many cases, that man will find what he needs from somewhere else.

What do I mean by "what he needs", let's allow Chris Jackson to share a sobering thought with you:

> *Here's the thing, I know a lot of men that are very successful and then they have some wives that are doing some incredible things. But yet every Friday, the guy is at the strip club. So what are they looking for at the strip club? Are they going to the strip club just to see naked women? No! They go to the strip club because they seek femininity. Typically a lot of women when they take on the role and the responsibility of masculine energy in the workplace they wear it throughout the day, and very few women know how to take that energy off when they cross the threshold of the home. So the idea of putting on lingerie is almost insulting to women. They {are} like, 'why should I have to do that? If anything he should be putting it on for me." So that right there is masculine energy...very few women know how to take that mask off when they walk across the threshold and be feminine and be what we think is this stereotypical and/or even the biblical terminology of a woman. I think one of the things that we lost in our society and in our culture is the essence of femininity. What exactly is that? How to seduce your man without touching them? How to use feminine energy to conquer the world? People don't realize that feminine energy has actually caused some of the greatest wars in the world. Some of the greatest wars were fought over a woman. Feminine energy can stop or start a war. That is the power of femininity and we don't teach that to women. Instead, we teach that if you're feminine then you are an airhead or you're weak. Femininity and being an airhead are two different things. An airhead is an airhead and says one plus one equals five, that's an airhead but the feminine woman knows how to play that whereas one plus one equals two and two equals me and you, and we can conquer this life together a lot better than us doing it individually.*

I'm laughing a little bit because I heard a lady say, "Yes, I am mouthy but I sex the hell out my man." I said to her, "well that's great but what happens when another woman comes along with your success level or better who knows how to balance that in a home? You think if he realizes he can have a successful woman and a respectful woman that he won't eventually think about leaving you for her? Men are not that smart when it comes to resisting the essence of another woman particularly if you leave him empty in an area where he is looking to be filled. Please, do not give him that much credit that he has the ability to keep turning that type of woman down. Ladies, my advice to you is to put a harness on your tongue. Your man is unable to handle emasculation.

There is absolutely nothing wrong with a woman being independent. Women can be as independent as they desire to be outside the home but please understand that you have a role to play at home as well. At home you are **INTERDEPENDENT**. You might be the leader at work, but you are not the leader in your home. Your man is the leader of the household. I understand that you might have had your own house, car, money and other amazing things you may have acquired but when you get married, you become **ONE**. You and your spouse become dependent on one another. "Mine and Yours" should no longer be the culture in a healthy marriage. Do not confuse independence with codependence. Your man is not expecting you to be weak or without an opinion but the culture of the home should be that of honor, respect and an assurance that both of your needs are being met.

Sam Smith said, *"if you marry the overly independent and strong person I think that you can run into some problems with the "mine" versus "yours".... if we moved into our household and we're engaged or married and you still have that mentality of "this is mine, this is my bank account, this is your bank account, and what I bring in this marriage is mine and what you bring in is yours," and "I don't want to lose my identity" Yes, we're going to share some things but you still have that separation, then that's wrong...we should be one in all things love, finances, the good times, the bad times, everything."*

At home, you are the COO, the Vice President, the Chief of Staff, and Second-In-Command. It does not mean that you are weak or that you should be "barefoot and pregnant". Please **STOP** listening to society's perspective about how a woman's role is the same as the man's role in the home. It's a lie. The truth is when a woman maximizes her role in the home, she becomes more powerful than the man. Men know this, we just don't say it. What society makes women think is that a man's role is better and stronger than a woman's role. Society influences women to act like men instead of empowering them to play their role well. It's the most backwards thing and that is a major contribution to the breakdown of the traditional family. We have women trying to be the leader in the home and displaying masculine energy when meanwhile, men are already dumb in a relationship. So you have the women acting like men, a man being a man, and now you have the blind trying to lead the blind. That's not going to work.

Another downfall that many independent woman face in marriage is the inability to be the proper helpmate for her man. When a man finds a wife, he has found a good thing and now has the potential to experience a lifetime full of blessings and favor. You know why that is? Because women have the ability to look at a man and see him for what he can be. Then over time as he begins to care and love her, he will grow deeper into executing on his talent. He then uses that talent to maximize the financial contributions for his family as well as become a better man over time. But here is the interesting part. A woman was designed to help her man give birth to his hidden talents. He was not designed to do it alone. Everyone knows that women have the ability to birth children, but the smart ones know that in addition to children, they also birth the man into becoming the best he can be. And that is why when a man finds a wife, he finds a good thing because THAT is the woman that will take him to the next level if she functions in her role correctly.

Can a man be great without a wife? Yes. But he will never be as great as he should be without adding that final piece to his life. A man has an idea and he comes to his woman and tells her that he needs help in its most basic form. Now "help" can come in different forms. It could be by simply being a sounding board or providing constructive feedback, helping him research or maybe tweak the idea. She may support him by keeping his head clear or not being negative about his idea even if she disagrees with it. But some women are so caught up in their role as Vice President of a company, or an Entrepreneur, that she rejects her role to help her man. She listens to society that says her goals, dreams and aspirations are more important than her husband's. She does not take the time to help him give birth to his idea, thus, leaving the man to maximize his potential alone. He may still achieve much success but he may resent his "helpmate" operating in her role and helping him get there. And here is the scary part ladies, somebody did help him, it just wasn't you. That doesn't mean that he cheated on you. It means that in his mind, you don't get the credit for helping him reach higher levels. The help could have come from his mother, sister, cousin, or maybe even one of his homeboys, or maybe it was a female friend. **But it wasn't you.**

Now, allow me to relieve some of the pressure to function in your role as a wife. You don't have to help birth his ideas. You don't have to speak respectfully to him. You don't have to take on the roles that are necessary to be an intentional wife and mother. The best way to do that is to not get married. **Marriage is not for everyone.** It's not for "Ms. Independent" that can "do life" all by herself. Stay in an uncommitted relationship. Have casual sex. Keep your bank account and other business matters separate and live your life without the responsibility of helping a man and successfully operating in your role in the home.

BUT if you want to get married, be mindful of these Empowerment Tools prior to saying **"I do."** If you are already married, make the adjustment today. Don't wait another moment to implement a new climate of INTERDEPENDENCE in the home. Remember, when a woman maximizes her role in the home, she becomes more powerful than the man...and he knew it when he found you.

Empowerment Tools:

- Do not emasculate your man, he is unable to handle masculine energy from you.
- Ask for wisdom and embrace your role as a partner and the unification of two people under one leader in your household.
- Help your man give birth to his ideas and watch your home and life flourish.

...there is a difference between enhancing and putting on a costume.

CHAPTER 3

We Didn't Tell You To Do All That!

THE UPKEEP OF someone's appearance is always important. Good hygiene, ironed clothes, smelling good, hair looking neat and the like, all of those things let people know that you are able to present yourself well. Women taking care of themselves inside and out is vitally important. Some women feel that enhancements to their bodies such as hair extensions, eyelashes, makeup, butt pads, breast enhancements and the like allow them to be more attractive. I enjoyed this interview topic with the gentleman as I wanted to reveal **how men feel about women adding certain enhancements to their bodies**. We also discussed the natural look as well as having a woman with enhancements being your wife opposed to being your girlfriend.

Men are perfectly fine with the nails and toes getting done. Obviously, if you wear sandals, you want to make sure the feet look presentable. Add a little lotion, and you should be good to go.

If you are attending an elegant affair such as a wedding or a black tie event, we understand that you may go the extra mile to do what you may feel will make you more attractive. We understand that's when you do the extra makeup, hairstyles, and eyelashes to enhance your overall look. I get it. We get it.

But ladies can I please help you save some money? The next time you are scheduled to attend an event with your mate, ask him does he care if you wear eyelashes. Ask him does it matter if you put hair extensions in. I guarantee that his answer will be, "no". The only reason he will say yes is because he thinks that's what you want and it makes you happy. But he really does not care. Now, there are some men who are adamant about women not adding any enhancements to their bodies, it's imperative that you tailor your look to what you are comfortable with and balancing it with what your man likes. If you want his approval or even a compliment, don't just go out and get it, get his opinion before spending money you don't have to spend on enhancements you don't have to have.

Are there some superficial men who want you to go the extra mile and add extra makeup, fake contacts and hair extensions? Yes, but the majority of us do not care for it. "She has the most beautiful eyelashes," is the one phrase I have never heard a man say. Women do not get compliments from men on their eyelashes because we are not looking at that.

Kevin Gray shares his views on eyelashes: *One of the things that I've noticed and women have been doing it for years but I've noticed particularly in the last year-and-a-half, are these fake eyelashes. What ends up happening is that I can see the glue on the eyelashes, the eyelashes are not on straight and I say to myself look you need to stop it. Your regular eyelashes are fine. Your natural you, is good enough. I don't even care about eyelashes and it turns me off and when it starts coming off and you can see the glue on it... that's not good...lol*

Can we talk about the weave and wig phenomenon? I remember seeing a post on social media from a woman who asked the question "**why do men have a problem with wigs?**" And the response was, **"well how would you feel if your man came home and hung his muscles up in the closet?"** Now I know you might see that as extreme, but there's no difference. Ladies, let me share something with you. If your man loves you, he won't really give a damn about your hair as long as it's neat and done, that's probably all that he cares about.

I love how Barry Case drives this point home about hair for his wife: *I do think you should look attractive... now what attractive is, is relative and it's subjective to the individual and what they like... For example one of the things I've seen over the years being with my wife when I was a younger man I had a traditional stereotypical thought process of what attractive women looked like. But over the years I have evolved because in the earlier part of our marriage I had her in a box, "you need to look like this and you need to do this"... through the years when I erased some of those boundaries and took some of the pressure off of her, and let her do her, I'm like "wow, you cut your hair...wow, you're going natural" and it's beautiful and sexy and I'm saying to myself "wow, I never would have thought of that... I thought the hair had to be long and come down, be permed... and over the years I'm just like wow she's beautiful...Beautiful women come in all shapes and sizes and the whole enhancement piece, I could really do without.*

When was the last time you asked your husband if you took the weave out, would he care? If he loves you, he will say, "No". If you notice, I keep saying "ask your husband if he cares" for a reason. Women spend so much money, time and effort, however, the first phrase you hear women say is, "I just want to look nice". Look nice for who? If you are married, the only person you should care about looking nice for other than yourself is your husband. No one else should matter. And if you are single, stay tuned, we're going to address this topic for you in a moment.

To be clear, most women do not get dressed up with the sole thought that their man will be happy with what they've chosen to wear. What he thinks may be a fraction of the thought, but generally speaking, women get dressed for other women. They're worried about what the other woman will say about their shoes, makeup, eyelashes, hair and the like. How crazy is that? Ladies, you are spending all that money for stuff we don't care about and we didn't tell you to go do any of that. Some women have conditioned their minds to think that what other women think looks nice, is what they should do to look nice. But if you are a heterosexual woman, shouldn't you be more concerned about what a man thinks versus another woman?

Here is something I find funny and sad at the same time. Women will wear makeup and/or hair extensions and/or eyelashes, fake contacts and the like and see another woman who they don't like or don't even know and with a straight face say, "I don't like her because she acts so fake….or she looks fake." I just look at them and say to myself, **"At what point did you miss the fact that the hair on your head is not the hair you were born with? Your face doesn't really look like that nor is that your real eye color."** This kind of phony behavior has become the norm and I understand it but please stop contradicting yourself by calling someone else fake.

Let's talk about breast enhancements for a moment. For the ladies who had to undergo a medical procedure in order to correct a problem due to an illness or discomfort, I can totally understand that. That was a medical procedure that you needed and you are excluded from this breast enhancement conversation.

Now let me be clear and say that I love women's breasts and I think they are a great creation from God. Here's something I have observed over the years with fake breasts. When you are young, they may look great. But when you get older, they may not look as good as they did when you were younger. What 60+ year-old woman do you know with perky breasts? Do they look natural? You be the judge. I want you to consider that as you make a decision regarding breast implants, just remember that getting older is inevitable. Somewhere along the line, society has tricked women into believing that big boobs make you more attractive. I don't agree. I think that whatever you were born with is what's beneficial for your body type. Sometimes when women undergo breast augmentation, it doesn't look natural. Most of the time you can tell who has them because you have this lady with a very thin frame but gigantic breasts. The most frustrating part about breast enhancements is women have the audacity to get mad if a man is talking to them and looking at their chest. Didn't you get the boobs for attention? Perhaps you got them to raise your self-esteem, but you have to take the good with the bad on this one. Also, I haven't felt fake boobs (that I know of), but I have heard many men say they don't like the way they feel.

Rodney Lawson addresses some of these same points by saying, "*...breast enhancements are a woman's brokenness, the unworthy, and/or the insecure feeling inside of the woman... so what they are looking to do, is enhance something else about them so they'll have more attraction or more men saying "well, she looks good... wow, she looks like this or that".... When it comes to a woman adding fake enhancements to their bodies, I do not like it. I don't like the way fake breasts feel. I have felt them and I don't like the way they feel... Those are not natural up against me... I'm very affectionate, I love to cuddle but I can't cuddle with things that are unnatural up against me. I don't mind the eyelashes and the makeup and a little hair but when you start messing with the internal stuff of your body it just does not feel natural to me.*"

Regarding butt pads and injections, you are making the dumbest move by doing that. I have yet to hear from one man who is cool with butt enhancements. The whole concept is a setup for failure. What is going to happen when you eventually take your clothes off and your guy sees you weren't being honest? Instead of you being natural and letting him make a decision if he wants to talk to you in your natural state, you tried to fool him into thinking your butt was bigger than it really was. Do you really qualify for a relationship with that man if you've been lying the entire time?

Poncho thinks women who use butt enhancements are lazy: *I'm not necessarily opposed to the enhancements for other parts of your body but let me say that butt shots I feel are flat-out lazy. You can go to the gym and get a membership and enhance your rear end. If you're going to enhance your rear end by getting shots, that just tells me that you don't want to put in the time and respect your body enough to go in and work for it ... and it's cool to look at but getting butt shots is discounting what the women are doing here in the gym every day, going and getting on the squat rack, and running and keeping themselves in shape. It's kind of a slap in the face to them... again it's cool to look at but I prefer them to be natural. The weave, makeup, the eyelashes, etc... I prefer a woman that does not need that. I'm okay with them wearing it but I prefer that they not need it... if they want to change the look up, I can understand but there is a difference between enhancing and putting on a costume.*

Let's explore the last sentence where Poncho said: **"there is a difference between enhancing and putting on a costume."** When you are adding enhancements to your body, you are putting on a deceptive costume. The definition of a costume is "a set of clothes, especially a woman's ensemble, for a particular occasion or purpose." The Ensemble that you put on is for the purpose of looking good and attracting someone else but it is not a representative of who you naturally are. But let's go deeper since I can feel the costume definition is giving you some excuses to continue dressing yourself up. So let's state for the record the following:

We agree the fake contacts are not your real eyes.
We agree the hair extensions are not your real hair.
We agree the lashes are not your eyelashes.
We agree the butt pads and injections are not your natural butt.
We agree the breast enhancements are not your natural breasts.

So let's sum this up with a few definitions:

Fraud = a person or thing intended to deceive others, typically by unjustifiably claiming or being credited with accomplishments or qualities; an act of deceiving or misrepresenting; one that is not what it seems or is represented to be.

Dishonest = means intended to mislead or cheat; behaving or prone to behave in an untrustworthy or fraudulent way.

Deception = means the act of causing someone to accept as true or valid what is false or invalid; the fact or condition of being deceived; something that deceives.

Trickery = means the practice of deception; the practice of crafty underhanded Ingenuity to deceive or cheat.

I'm sure you may not like these definitions, but they represent what you are doing when you alter your appearance for the public. When you go outside with a wig or weave, you are committing an act of deception or misrepresenting what your hair really is. That by definition is a fraud. Although society has made you think differently about eyelash extensions you are committing the act of causing someone to accept as true what your eyelashes really look like and that can be a condition of deception. When you put those butt pads on or take butt injections, you are utilizing crafty underhanded ingenuity to deceive a man about the size of your butt, which is trickery. When you get breast enhancements, you are misleading men about the true size of the breasts you were born with which is a form of dishonesty. Are you a fraud? Are you being dishonest? Are you deceiving men and utilizing trickery to seduce them? When did that become okay to do in life?

If your man did not come home last night and he does not tell the truth about where he was that makes him a liar, right? It doesn't matter why he lied, he still lied. My point is, every time you change your natural appearance, you are telling a lie. What I find most interesting is that women hate a man who lies, but yet they get dressed and walk out the door and lie to the world all day long about their real appearance. Most women want a man who's honest, trustworthy and loyal but you want a pass to lie every day about who you really are? Ladies, here's the thing: when we roll over in the morning and find out what you really look like or when we discover the person that we met is not the person that we thought you were from an appearance perspective, we do not like it.

Rassi: *I don't really want to wife you if you are wearing weave and contacts... I'm not doing none of that because none of that is attractive to me. I don't like weave. I don't like long ass hair that isn't yours, ending up on me somewhere... I'm squeamish...I mean if you got to put in a little more enhancements every now and then because you have somewhere to go and it calls for long hair and all that, then that's cool.... but if that's your every day, every time I see you thing... you rocking it like you the sh** because of it? No, ma'am... I mean I do know some dudes that do care about it... I know one guy that he won't mess with anybody but a stripper and you know how they rocking all types of enhancements.... that's just not something I'm into. I'm more into Natural Women.*

Other than the comment that came from Barry Case, throughout this chapter I intentionally used quotes from some of the single men whom I interviewed. I wanted you to see in particular that many single men would much rather you be honest... excuse me... **natural.** So for the single ladies, here's the part that I want you to take heed to; Men want to see upfront what they are getting involved with regarding your appearance just like you want to hear the truth from us when you first meet us. Unfortunately, some of you may feel that my comparisons are extreme. I would like you to know that you are making excuses so you can continue the behavior just like a man will make an excuse for why he needs to lie to you. The more you lie, the more you will be lied to.

I hope that most of you picked up on a recurring word that most of the men were saying, "natural." I want you to understand the importance of the word natural. You are beautiful because God created you. When you look in the mirror, you should be thankful for what God has made. If you want to make some changes, research the most organic way to do so. Take a vitamin and/or do some exercises. If you are single and you think you are lacking in an area that makes you less attractive, please stop thinking like that. You are enough. You are good enough to attract the man that God has made for you. Spend less time in the mirror and more time working and enhancing the God-given talent that is inside of you. When you operate inside of that talent, you will be sent the man created just for you.

Stop allowing society to convince you to spend money on things that ultimately do not matter to most men. **We didn't tell you to do any of that because it's not what we want.** We want you in your most organic and authentic state. The natural woman you were originally made to be is who we want to be in love with. In order to do that, we need your understanding that from day one we want you to present to us who you are, not who "they" say you should be.

<u>Empowerment Tools:</u>

- Ask your man does he really care about the enhancements you may add to your body
- Spend less time in the mirror and more time working and enhancing the God-given talent that is inside of you
- There is a difference between adding enhancements to your body and putting on a costume. Keep it real with us at all times, we can handle it.
- Allow a man to make the decision of accepting you in your natural state from the very beginning

You must determine very early in your encounters with this man if you are dealing with a boy or a man.

Chapter 4

Do You See Me?

Oftentimes, women feel that men like to be private and not allow a woman into his thoughts and life. Some men feel if she gets to know him, she can help take him to the next level. The gentlemen I interviewed discussed how men really want women to get to know them, and not just know things about him, but know who he actually is. "**What can a woman do, to get to know you, without seeming like she is pushy or trying to be "all in your business" too soon or at all?**

We discussed earlier in this manual about a woman's checklist. Many men think women always have some kind of hidden agenda when they become interested in a man. Whether its commitment or a future family, women have a tendency to begin to lead a man down a path of a relationship once they become interested in him. What helps with this process is knowing what you want. But here is the scary part about this, as we've discussed earlier with regards to your checklist, this is simply knowing what direction you want to take and the type of things you want in your relationship. At this point, the song by Lauryn Hill keeps playing in my mind. The statement that she made in the song is "How you gon' win when you ain't right within?" Let me give you the translation of this verse: how are you going to begin a relationship when you don't even know what you want for yourself? When you know what you want, the early stages of your relationship become a lot easier. It creates less heartache down the road and allows the person you are looking to build a relationship with to either move forward with you or find someone else.

Charles addresses this first phase of the relationship by saying: "*Women have the gift of the ability to ask the right questions. I think that if you're going to get to know somebody, ask the right questions. Find out what you need to find out using wisdom. When I say using wisdom, I mean that the more and more that you learn about who you are, and about what you want, and what God wants for you, and the more you care about how your words are received, you will ask the question in a way that expresses love and respect. You will also come from a side of "this is what I need to know in order to make a certain decision." For example, if I want to know how a woman thinks about marriage, I'll say "hey, what do you think that it means to be a wife?" So now I leave it open for her to talk. And often times with people, if you give them a broad enough question, they will give you all of the information that you need to know. If you just let people talk, and you listen.... I think that if a woman wants to get to know a man, she asks the right questions, and she watches his actions. A man is based on what he does, not necessarily what he says.*

You have the ability to uncover what direction your man is headed in by asking the right questions. Will you be right all the time? Maybe not. The point is, the more you learn about yourself, personally develop yourself, and put your feminine qualities to work on understanding your potential mate, the faster you'll be able to determine if you should continue to invest time into this relationship or terminate it.

So now that you have the understanding of the first important phase of knowing what you want in a relationship, the next phase would be to determine what type of man you are dealing with. Many times the male species can become resistant or come off like he is not ready to be in a committed relationship. Sometimes we can appear private by not allowing a woman to get too close. One of the main reasons a man may behave this way stems from him "being hurt" by another woman from a previous relationship. Having been there before, I want to share **Two Principles** about the, **"I've been hurt before"** statement so that women can understand it.

Principle #1 If a man has been hurt by a woman in a previous relationship, all you want to do is acknowledge it, and then file it in the back of your mind. The reason why I say file in the back of your mind is because although the man might be sensitive about his past, that has nothing to do with you. We all have been there and have experienced disappointments in our lives. And just like with any other challenge, he has to learn to move on. **That is not your project.** You as a woman have somewhere you are ordained to be in a relationship with a man.

If you let his thoughts of his past cripple your plight of where you want to go, then that is your fault. My advice here will be play this early stage by ear, but if he is deep in his past when you are discussing your future, be cautious and make the judgment call to either stick it out or move on. Do this early. Do not waste your time on anyone who is caught up in their past.

Principle #2 You must determine very early in your encounters with this man if you are dealing with a boy or a man. Boys get hurt, dwell on the past, and use the past to possibly rob them of their future blessings. On the contrary, men understand that life can bring a multitude of challenges to include hurtful breakups. We also know that past relationships are to be learned from and utilized to enhance lives and add blessings to our future. As a woman, you need to determine if you are dealing with a wounded boy or progressive man. A man is able to look at you and see the blessing that you can be. He also knows that if he is going to move forward with you, he has to begin to let you into his mind and his world if he has plans to embark on a committed relationship.

Rafiq says, "*...she's going to have to quickly determine whether she's dealing with a boy or with a man. The reason why I say that is because it's difficult to get to know a boy... and there are a lot of grown boys that are out there and when I say boy I want to make a clear delineation that there's a maturity level that's in place that's different between a boy and a man. With a boy, you're going to get a lot more ego, you're going to get a lot more facade, you're going to get a fake confidence, and that type of person is not really going to try to let you in to let you know just how fake their game really is. But if you talking about a man, then this is when the woman has to use her feminine power. What comes with manhood is the trials and tribulations of life that transition a boy into a man and that kind of man has been through some things and came out on the other end. He may not have swag, but he's got confidence.. that type of person is much more open to a woman getting to know who they are because she's not going to hit a level of him and say "oh wow there's nothing else" as with a boy you start digging and then see there's nothing else there... but a man has complexity. He's got layers and it's something that's attractive and appealing to a woman to try to get to those layers and peel back the onion. Have you ever seen a tree that has been cut down? When you look at the tree on the inside, you can see all the rings. Each ring represents the progressive years of the aging of the tree. That man is just like a tree. There are lots of rings that were formed from the hardship and pain and struggle, and that person is usually much more open* *because he's secure about who he is. So he'll say "come on in and get to know me...come on in and get to know these rings in here."*

Ladies, if you choose to hang in there and peel back the layers, understand that you must have patience. I'm not going to tell you how long this process can take, but I will say that your discernment on whether you are dealing with a boy or a man should happen fairly quickly. Now, that doesn't mean 24 hours, one week, or a month. It also doesn't mean one to two years either. Use your God-given ability and pray for understanding and patience, but **don't be a fool.** You normally can discern early on whether he is worth sticking it out or not.

Let's imagine that you've gone through the early stages and now you want to take things to the next level. I'm going to give you one of the fastest ways to get a man to yield to you and in your direction: Find out what his goals are and what he likes to do in his spare time. Don't worry about being around his family or friends just yet. Are his family and friends important to know about? Yes, but don't start thinking too deeply about that yet. If you do this next step correctly, you will find that he will proactively have you in the presence of any and every one who is meaningful to him without you ever asking him to do so.

Delante touches on this next phase by saying, *"She needs to figure out how to implement herself in my life. It's about time and knowing when, and where, and how to implement herself. It's very self-involved but most women can find their way into the puzzle. For example, she can think to herself "I know he's going to be in this area and he may be in this kind of mood" and then she figures her way into my life, and after a while it will become so consistent until when you're not around, the guy is going to say to himself "so why is she not here?" That's how she would have to get to know me, and where I am as a man today. Take a look at my life, and figure out how to insert yourself inside of it, and as you do that, you're going to get to know me...I have not had great experiences with women hunting me...she comes [on] too strong. For example, let's say a woman is interested in you and she gives you a call. She'll say, "I just happened to have made a turkey and I know it's not Thanksgiving....and...I made this soufflé and I had to go to Lowe's and get a torch burner to get the crust right... but anyway I really didn't have anything to do and if you're hungry I'll stop by"... and I feel like I'm not going to eat your poisoned meat..... and that's how I honestly feel.. It's weird to me and that's too aggressive hunting and that's too obvious. It's cool for Netflix and Chill, but when its dating and you're trying to set it up like you got some food, movie, and what we're going to do at night... it makes me feel weird... so that doesn't work for me...*

Ladies, please understand that if you do this phase correctly, you will begin to see your potential man do one of two things: He will either draw closer to you or you will know that you need to terminate the relationship. Why is it so simple? Because of what Delante said earlier. If he is feeling you, once he lets you into his world and opens up, it will give you all the knowledge you need to say whether or not you will continue to entertain him or not.

Now, let me caution you ladies. This does not mean that you become aggressive on inserting yourself into his life. Don't call him every day like "what are you doing? Can I come with you today, tomorrow, this weekend?" But be more subtle. Be available but not desperate. Be interested but not fake about his interests. Be a helper when you see how you can enhance his world, but don't try to change his world. As you continue to show interest, he will continue to pull you in more and more. He will begin to invite you to be around the people who are important to him such as friends and family. This will further help you make a decision a lot sooner on whether or not his world is somewhere you see yourself being a part of. This is also the time you begin to expose more of your world to him along with your likes and dislikes. As you do this, you will be able to see whether his world is congruent with your world which will help you determine whether or not to continue with this particular relationship.

You don't have to move fast, but you need to be tactical. Use your grace, at the right pace, and you will finish the race with the right man by your side. Here is an echo of Delante's words with a few pointers for this phase in the relationship.

Trey Barnette advises, *"I would say take it easy... don't go from 0 to 100 real quick. Women need to take it in steps and strides and I think it's all about presentation. Number 1, get to know who I am. Get to know what I'm about and get to know what makes me tick as a person. Understand who your mate is and how to relate to him. That comes from asking questions. That comes from going on activities together and having experiences together. Even if you don't like to play a game of pickup basketball, go out there and try because that's what your man likes to do.. If you don't like to lace up and run, see if you can run a quarter of a mile. You're not doing it for you, but you're trying to experience those things with that mate. The second thing is get to understand what that person's world is around them... Their co-workers their friends. Do they have kids? Family? What is their world [like] around them? The ways you can do that is by putting yourself in a position where you experience those things. I'm not talking about pop up at poker night. I'm not talking about invite yourself to the family reunion... I'm talking about as the person is talking about those things to you, see if there's a possibility of you being a part of those things. The third thing would be goals... what are your goals in life and what is your man's goals in life and do they align with each other?... don't try to force something... don't force the square peg in the round hole... if it doesn't fit you must acquit and get out the relationship... lol... if it doesn't fit get out that relationship and do it early... stop the bleeding. Now after the goals THEN the next step would be okay, if I go down the line and our family values align okay what would life be together with each other? What I find is women go 0 to 100... The guy says "Hi, my name is Bob" and she's like "okay, babe...hey, do you want to have kids?" and we're like "Whoa!... hey, relax...be easy." And that's where a lot of women shoot themselves in the foot......they don't want to get to know who this man is and it's really about them just jumping the gun. Women need to bring back game...need to get to the women who were smooth and knew the right thing to do and say and how to sex a man down the right way without even touching him... where is the swag with these women?... they don't have any swag anymore."*

I want to overemphasize this phase with multiple examples for one reason, this is the phase where you will be able to actually draw the line on anything that you may not like that you have witnessed in his world. In this phase, he is showing you who he is. He is saying to you, "do you see me? Do you like what you see? Can you hang with what you see?" He is also saying, "If you don't like what you see, then you might need to leave."

Now, please understand that just like Rassi said earlier about **The 80-20 Rule**, this is when the ball is in your court. Whatever nuances that you've witnessed in his world that you truly find repulsive, or a deal-breaker, this is when you can be honest with him and say, "I like you and I see a future with us, but I cannot see myself embracing XYZ." Here's a newsflash: If you did Phase 3 correctly, the man may resist for a moment, but by this time he's now seeing the value you've added by being in his world. He will either begin to take the steps to make his world more acceptable for you, or he will not. Simple as that. If he chooses not to make the adjustment, as Trey said earlier, that's when you leave. And here is the crazy part, if you did Phase 3 correctly, and he sees you backing away from him or notices you have actually checked out of the relationship, he will recognize what he is about to lose and come running back to you.

Rassi wraps this chapter up with this point: *"Getting to know me takes a good amount of patience and understanding. I'm simple on the outside but I'm a complex individual on the inside. If you're getting to know the real me and if you're not ready to accept what I've already told you as me and you send a representative of yourself to act as if you accept me but then the real you doesn't, then there's a problem there. I would like for somebody to really get to know me and to accept me, but I'm not sure that women are able to handle what they hear when their man tells them who they really are. I'm an open book at the beginning of a relationship because I don't want you to come back and say that I gave you a different representative of myself. I want them to know that I'm giving you the real me and it's going to be consistent throughout so that if something down the line happens, you don't say I never let you know that I would be like this.... No... I did tell you, you just chose to ignore it, and you chose to think that you can change me, but this is the real me, and always has been.*

This chapter is crucial because it involves being a woman. This is where the rubber meets the road with regards to you maximizing your feminine qualities. You might ask, "What does he mean by being a woman? I'm already a woman." I say to you that a vagina does not make you a woman, no different than a penis makes a man. Those body parts are on boys and girls. A woman has to utilize her feminine qualities to properly execute on acquiring the right man in her life and build a lasting relationship with him. This takes knowledge of herself, her worth, and her ability to receive the right man for her life. If you don't know who you are as a woman or know your worth, it does not make you a bad person. It just means that right now you may not need to be in a relationship until you're able to fully understand who you really are. After you understand who you are, only then can you understand a man and build a relationship with a man.

Lastly, I want to emphasize what Charles said earlier by, **"Watch his actions and not his words."** Let me make this last point simple. If a man shows you who he is in Phase 3, believe him. Do not try to change him by nagging or constantly complaining about his actions. Now this doesn't mean that you should be silent and not address an issue that you've noticed. You can address it once, maybe even twice. After that, make a decision. Go back to Phase 3, and address it the way I stated. The problem is that women are too scared to stand up and be firm about their deal-breakers. Maybe you love him by now, or maybe you fear being alone, or "getting back out there" into the dating game, so you ignore your concerns or think to yourself "maybe I can change him." And guess what? That is the wrong move. We know through your words over time whether you fear addressing that which is unacceptable to you and why you fear losing us by settling for whatever nuances we have. We will remain in the relationship as long as we can before making the decision to adapt to whatever it is that you want changed or letting you keep dealing with us until you finally decide to leave us. And here's the kicker, if we know we will never change it, we are already in the market for your replacement, you just don't know it.

Empowerment Tools:

Phase 1 - Know what you want from the relationship and what direction you want to take with him

Phase 2 - Quickly identify if he is a boy or man.

Phase 3 - Insert yourself into his world gracefully. Pay attention and make the determination if this is someone you can continue to grow with or not.

Phase 4 - Don't try to change what you've learned in Phase 3. Make a decision to allow God to fix his flaws or move on.

...men would rather go off by themselves than to deal with a nagging woman.

Chapter 5

What Is Nagging?

By now, you've read that I've interviewed twenty-four men from different backgrounds and various life experience. The topics that we have been discussing originated from each one of us in some shape or form. Each of the men shared three to five topics that they wanted women to understand about them. Can you guess which topic was in the top 3? **Nagging.** Clearly, this is an element we would like to help you understand and cease in your relationship.

When I pondered the notion of nagging, the first thought that came to mind is this should be one of the shortest chapters in the entire manual. Why must we have a conversation about nagging? Why do we even need to give any understanding as to why women need to pay attention to this? But as I went back and looked at some of the data that I've collected, as well as thought further about the matter, my mind shifted. This topic is extremely critical for **3 reasons.** If you nag your man he:

- may **not** want to come home to you.
- may spend less time with **you**.
- may spend less time around **your children**.

Now you might say, "That's crazy! How could a man not want to be around his children just because the woman is nagging?"

I asked the men, "**What is nagging to you and how does it make you feel?**" Then I went on to ask them, **"How do you think a woman should request something and then follow up without it being considered nagging?"**

Nagging is the constant harassing of someone to do something; persistently, painfully and/or in a worrisome manner. An ancient proverb reveals, *"It is better to dwell in the wilderness than with a contentious and an angry woman."* In other translations of the ancient proverb, it reports, *"It is better for a man to dwell on the rooftop than to deal with a contentious and angry woman."* Is it true that a man would rather live on the rooftop of his house than deal with a woman who specializes in nagging? He would rather go off into the wilderness? Do you know what the 'rooftop' and 'wilderness' look like? They are metaphors for a man wanting to be anywhere else other than near a nagging woman. And if he's not near you, there is a chance he will not be near the family either. For those of you who thought it was absurd about a man not wanting to be around you nor the children, you can now begin to see that even from the beginning of time, men would rather go off by themselves than to deal with a nagging woman.

Here's feedback from 5 different men about the problem with nagging:

Porter Bingham: *I would define nagging as a wife approaching you with concerns repetitiously in a manner that is less than cooperative and dictating to you and anything that leads to emasculation and picking out a negative of whatever they are trying to accomplish. Usually, they have an objective and it's not malicious but it's just the way that the woman is communicating. Women like security and if they feel like their security is threatened then they're going to constantly remind you of the things that they feel that you may be missing or you are short on and they're going to say things that will reinstate that security. We don't want to hear it over and over and over again, but a lot of that is the woman's inability to communicate with him effectively.*

Ryan Green: *Nagging makes me feel disrespected because I'm a fixer and most men are... if you come to me with a problem or with the request of something that you want and I say "okay, I'm going to take care of it", that's the end. Let me take care of it within my time frame... but if I thought I told you I was going to fix it and you keep coming back to me and asking me am I going to do it, now that's when it becomes nagging because you're constantly complaining to me about it. It seems to me like you don't want my help, you just want to complain about something and that's how I see it. I think a lot of times women begin to start nagging because they want something done their way and they don't respect a man to do it in his way... I think the nagging comes in because you didn't do it her way or you can't fix it her way.*

Telley Gilliard: *I'm actually in the room with my spouse right now and we actually talked about nagging earlier. How I would define nagging is that feeling that you have to tell me what I already know to do. For example, I know the garbage is full, I'm going to take it out, I don't need to take it out right then and there because you said it needs to... sometimes it might need to be pushed down so I can get a little bit more garbage in there...or "did you lock the doors? .... I'm like, "No baby, every night I want somebody to come in here on us." She asks me that every night. "Did you lock the door dear? I say, Yes dear."...dang it!!!...*

Chancey King: *Nagging to me is the consistent and the repetitive addressing of failure. If you're consistently reminding me of what I've done well, then that's not nagging. If you're consistently adding and speaking of the positive things that I'm doing and my nature of providing, then that's not nagging, that's building me up... but reminding me of my failures and my negatives that is nagging... and the thing is, I already know those, so I don't need to be reminded about them.*

Donald Bell: *It has been a challenge in our relationship of finding a delicate balance. Nagging is not necessarily about the content of what you're requesting. Nagging for most men is about the approach. Nagging is about the raising of the voice and the disrespect.... Women can get a response out of men without being negative, it's just all about the approach....a woman could have the cure to cancer, but if I don't like the way that you're saying it, I don't want to listen to what you have to say.*

What I've noticed in their responses is a universal message, your approach is everything. Most of us do not have an issue with what you have asked us to do but when you address us with a negative tone on top of constantly repeating the same issue, we feel emasculated and disrespected. We are unable to receive the message you are attempting to share with us because we are unable to process what you are saying due to your posture while saying it.

Before we go any further with solutions, allow me to pose two questions to you: **Why do you nag your man and why is it you have not found a better way to communicate your requests to him?** While you are thinking about your answers, allow me to share with you what I've noticed. The single men were not as knowledgeable about this topic as the married men. The recurring response among the single men was, **"I ignore ALL nagging women"**. Ladies, it's just that simple.

When I think back to my dating days, that's the same thing I used to do... IGNORE ALL NAGGING. Some of you may think the single guys aren't living with someone, but that's not always the case. Most of the men living with their significant other vehemently rejected all nagging. I lived with my wife for 8 to 9 months prior to getting married and I would ignore her, too. Married ladies, as we move toward better approaches rather than nagging, I challenge you to ask yourself, "**At what point did nagging become a better solution for me versus respectfully communicating with him?**

Donald Bell poses a good question: *"If you are looking to accomplish a goal, be it big or small, set the stage so that the ultimate goal can be met easier through productive conversation and communication....if you are saying to yourself, "people don't always talk like that" or "I don't have time to choose my words correctly every time..." My statement to you is "so you chose this man to marry, and you want him to think of you as his world and his everything...but you can't speak to him correctly...or choose your words correctly? Why is negative communication a norm for you and/or more comfortable versus it being out of the ordinary? What type of environment did you grow up in or who coached you that nagging is ok?"*

Ladies, it's all about your word choice, the tone of your voice and your posture while addressing your man. Look at nagging with the notion that **"you can catch more flies with honey, then you can with vinegar."** Throughout this chapter, we have discussed "the vinegar" or emasculating approach and its results, now let's discuss "the honey" or best approach for you man.

Rafiq who has been married twice said, *"I was with women who knew how to use their feminine powers to move me. I don't think that nagging is a good use of feminine power... and as soon as you say feminine power most people think that you're talking about sex because that's the power some think that women have over a man that she has to use... I'm not talking about that. I'm saying that a woman can move a man with dialogue if she knows her role. If she knows how to use her feminine power, she can move him like a chess piece all day long through the art of conversation... now that's a real woman. A girl or an immature woman is going to try to move you through sex or try to move you through control and she feels that sex is control and that's how she's going to move you. That's an immature woman because the real woman can move you in a... healthier way.*

Ladies, you have the ability to move your man through positive dialogue. If you are looking to accomplish a goal wouldn't it make more sense to use a less abrasive approach? The feminine power you have makes your man say to himself, "I want to satisfy her, so let me do what she's asked of me". Your power is so strong that he would even do exactly what he doesn't want to do just to make you happy. Knowing this powerful information, use your power for good. Just like a superhero, be the "Wonder Woman" of your household by possessing and utilizing the power to communicate effectively and get the results you need **without nagging.**

Now there are times when you will need to ask us to do something repeatedly no matter how respectful your approach has been. These are ways you can implement to respectfully ask him or follow-up with him effectively without nagging him:

Chancey offers two great suggestions*: "There are two things that have worked for me that I've noticed: Number one, if she knows that he hasn't done something, bring it up in a manner of reminding and how you can assist him to complete the task to make sure that he gets it done. For example, 'Hey, I noticed that you haven't gotten the car tags yet, do you need me to make sure that I leave the registration out on the table so that you'll be able to remember and not forget?'...or just anything simple that you can add to the effort of him completing the task. It might be something simple as taking something out of the drawer and putting it on the dresser where his keys are. Something simple that will help change his focus. And the second thing is to ask, 'if you can't do it then is it ok if I do it?'... and the average guy is going to say in his head or out loud to you "Hey, I said I was going to do it, I'm going to do it... I'm going to get it done because I don't want you to have to do it…" the average guy is not going to want his woman to do something that he told his wife that he was going to do and he knows that it is his responsibility... so the moment that the average guy is going to hear that, he is going to kick in gear... now there are a few of us that just don't care, ...but for the most part, the average guy is going to kick in and step up and do what he needs to do to complete the task.*

Porter Bingham*: I think they can bring it up, "Hey, this is a concern I have. How do you feel about it? ... Have you thought about how we might deal with it?" If the answer is 'No' okay... "Well, when you think about it let's circle back and talk about it", and leave it alone as opposed to "you're a procrastinator"... or "you're this or that"...or "we've got to deal with this mess!".... For a man that may constantly be on the go, you can follow up in this manner, just wait until the house burns down and then maybe he'll change the lightbulb.... but seriously if it's something essential to the way that you live, you mention it to him... For example, with my wife I'll be standing there one day and I'll look and see the light is out and she looks at me and says "Hey, I told you to change the lightbulb"..... and that's cool, and you can joke about that and move on. That's not ideal either, but sometimes men learn by empirical learning... so you mess around and light bulbs go out and the water gets cut off and then he can have a different level of respect the next time it comes around... lol.*

On behalf of the busy, unorganized, forgetful men in the world, I would like to apologize to all the women who have ever had to ask a man to do something more than once. We do not mean to be rude. Yes, your thoughts and the action you want us to do matters to us. We care about the family. We love you and the family, too, but sometimes things may slip our minds. One of the reasons is because men are not good multi-taskers. This sentiment should enlighten you as well as release you from the pressure and the stress of thinking you can ever change your man into a great multi-tasker. If you think you still can, good luck with that. For all the rest, let's look at some more techniques to help improve your man's propensity to get things done.

Brian Clarke shares a great collaboration established by he and his wife. *"I will go by what my wife does now which is she has figured out what works and what gets me to move. For example, she'll ask me to do something and I won't get it done... So she'll say. "Hey, babe have you done such and such yet?" and I'm like "no, I have not"... she'll ask me again "dude, have you done XYZ?" and I say, "No, baby I haven't done it yet, I'm sorry"... after about the third time she'll say "hey, this is what we're going to do, baby, I'm going to give you until this date and if it's not done then I'm going to go ahead and knock it out and do it" and I say, "ok."...99% of the time, that will get me to do it and I'll get it done before the deadline that she said. I work best with deadlines because I always have some things going on and so my wife has figured out to give a deadline and it works. Case and point in the last couple weeks, she wanted me to get the carpet cleaned and so she said "have you called the carpet guy yet" and I'll be like "no" and she'll say "listen I'm giving you until Thursday of next week to get it done, if not then I'll get it done"... That was a Saturday, and you best believe by that Wednesday it was done, and it was cool. It wasn't a nag it was just like, "hey, you know what I'm trying to do something that works for us" and that's what works for me and she has tapped into and observed me enough to see what works and what doesn't and the things that work, it works well... so now certain things that we found work for us, it's now our norm, and so this way she doesn't get frustrated and she calls it "not setting me up"... she's learned not to set her husband up[for failure]...*

What's great about this answer from Brian is that he shows how he is vulnerable to forgetting tasks requested by his wife. Brian is an attorney so naturally, he has a busy day. What's great about what his wife did is similar to what Chancey said as well. Brian's wife observed his challenge with time and used his ego to make him move without emasculating him. The reason this is important is because women already know the male ego is a sensitive area. If you speak negatively as it relates to our ego, it feels like disrespect and emasculation. But if you learn to use ego as a driving force, it will motivate us. This is a classic example of feminine power channeled correctly and communicated in a manner that made him say, "I've got to get this done." And ladies that's all you want the love of your life to do is get it done.

I want to give this last example and say that it is one of the best from a visual perspective. As Brian said earlier, his wife observed him and tried different things. My challenge to you is to find what works best for you and your spouse. Some men can receive verbal communication of a task and move forward with carrying it out. Others may need the verbal, plus a visual update or task list in order to complete what you are requesting.

A great idea from Sam Smith's family: *From experience, I would say write down what needs to be done. For example in my house, we have a chalkboard and whatever task is needed, is written down on the board. I know to look at the board and I mark them off as we go. The board is located in the foyer area of our home and everybody can see it. Depending upon if it's an event that I have to show up to, it's also put on the shared online calendar as well...and to be honest, anybody can put anything on that calendar in the house. At that point, if you've told me a specific time that something needs to be done and I have not completed it, then you can simply follow up by asking me about the particular event or subject that I was supposed to be taking care of. I am now accountable for your concern as to why it has not been done because you properly communicated to me what needed to be done, and what time, and I have not done it.*

And that's when you can be ignorant and go off on him...lol.

I'm just joking. I love the use of the visual task list on the chalkboard, but best of all it's the digital shared calendar usage that I can appreciate. That's something that my wife and I utilize as well. One quick entry to my calendar or an invite for dates and tasks that have to be completed is all I need to help me get things accomplished. Think about it ladies, many of you use calendars at work for accountability, right? Try that same approach at home. You can even customize the reminder notifications. You can set it up so he can receive as many reminder notifications as you desire via his phone or computer prior to the date that you want the task to be completed.

Ultimately, whatever technique you choose to implement, your goal is to get your man to complete a task. We have identified that **nagging will not help the situation.** The only recourse you have is to engage in a higher level of positive communication to accomplish any task and to choose a more positive approach. Remember ladies, this man is supposed to be the love of your life so set him up to win by actively helping him to complete your requests.

Empowerment Tools:

- Nagging doesn't move us and we despise it.
- Set clear expectations for the task
- Remember that men aren't good multi-taskers but you have the feminine power to guide him
- Find what reminder works best for him and implement it
    - Verbal
    - Verbal and visual
    - Digital
    - All of the above

"...When you tell your business, please keep in mind that the story will be exposed to someone else."

Chapter 6

Just Between Us

Marriage is not for everyone. Yes, it has wonderful moments filled with love, laughter, and joy, but anyone who has been married for any length of time will tell you that it can also have its ugly moments. It is during these times that we may inherently lean on friends and family as a sounding board and perhaps for advice from time to time. Friends and family are important and they are often the people who have been through the good and bad times with us. If there was a piece of advice that I wish I had more understanding of before I got married it would be the topic we will now discuss. When you're finished reading this chapter, please connect with someone who is thinking about getting married or perhaps a newlywed couple and tell them about this chapter. I was excited when I saw this as a topic the men wanted to talk about because we have a lot of wisdom to share with you.

The question posed to the men is twofold: **What are your thoughts about you or your spouse involving others in your marriage and can you give an example of your experience when you or your spouse have involved others in your marriage?**

The initial factor that needs to be understood is the sanctity and privacy that a marriage should have. You are two individuals brought together by God and the information that is shared about your home is sacred. Let's explore some of the possible outcomes that may occur when we expose our marriage life to others.

Chris Jackson says, *"I can really sum this question in one sentence. I heard it best from Tony Robbins. Whenever two people join together there is a third world that is formed. Whatever happens in that third world between those two people's minds is nobody else's business.*

I think that small example speaks to my relationship and the relationship that other people should have in their marriages as well. The only other person that is involved in that world is God. One of the things that people do in their relationship is that they feel like they have to bounce things off of others about their relationship and that to me is a sign of self-doubt. It's one of those things that you didn't conquer early on before you got married because when you get married that's probably one of the toughest things you'll ever do mentally and physically. It can be draining and it requires a lot of attention and sacrifice and if you haven't self-actualized by that point in life, then you're going to have some problems. You cannot allow too many voices and too many people into your relationship.

Porter Bingham advised, "*I think the question says it all. The relationship between you and your wife is incredibly sacred. So I keep people out at all costs. It's not something that's on the menu for general practice even with close family and friends. And that's what we've done over the years and it's worked out very well. I've never had a situation with my in-laws in my business or family was in our business and the way we've done it has served to protect the integrity of our relationship and also the relationship with our in-laws as well.*

I think these two gentlemen are giving the best advice about this topic. In a perfect world or an emotionally disciplined world, what they are saying is ideal. Unfortunately, for most of us, we try our best to keep people out of our relationships, but sometimes we find ourselves in some way speaking about the challenges that we may be facing in our marriages. When you make a decision to step outside of that sacred space, you put yourself and your marriage in a position where others may capitalize or take advantage of your situation.

In James Foulke's home, he has implemented the following strategy, "…*I keep[my personal business] very watered-down with no details if I do talk to anyone. The first thing is when you are having people know your business, you never know when they might tell somebody else what they should not be saying... so if there is a case that I do share some information with somebody, I'll let them know that this information is just for you and not for anybody else... and that's if I ever say anything... and it's not to be repeated and I make it clear that this information is not to be shared, rather than having it as an inference. I would never want anybody to speak about something that they should not be talking about with regards to my marriage. But in general, I find that people enjoy seeing other people not in a good place and I think that tends to be human nature...we have to fight against that... so giving somebody bad news when they are not doing so well sometimes makes other people feel better and I don't want to be a part of that.*

It's sad but true how some people like to hear bad news. Some people like to know that you are not doing well. And some people will tell your business. Everyone always has one other person that they share juicy stories and gossip with. When you tell your home business, please keep in mind that the story will be exposed to someone else. I know from personal experience that this is a very embarrassing and painful situation to be in.

Not only will involving others in your marriage put you in a situation of having your information shared with others, you also expose the possibility of someone capitalizing on you or your spouse's weaknesses. When I was dating my wife, we worked in a call center environment together. The one thing that I tell her today that we both laugh at is every time we got into an argument, she became my biggest fan for exposing me to other women. She would either tell someone that she was angry with me or somehow the other women in the call center could detect that she was upset with me. That was like ringing a dinner bell to the other women to come get me and I took full advantage of it every time.

Porter Bingham: *I've never seen anything positive come out of a situation when people have shared their relationship with family and friends... but I have seen the negative things. We all have problems or shortcomings and typically when you sit down and you want to talk to your friend about a problem that you might be having, there are a couple things I've seen that happen with other people... one of those things you have to keep in mind is that you might not be the only person that likes your spouse....when you start telling other people about some of the problems that you have at home, then that can also open the door for other people to slip in and cannibalize your relationship. I've seen that and I've seen it in my relationship... my wife is a social butterfly and I don't think she exposes our relationship to other people, but there are people who have been in our lives as friends that have sensed when something was wrong...Females, in particular, take advantage of it and that's a glaring example of and at the top of the list of things to not do.*

Ladies, please remember that women may want your man or husband. When you confide in others or in a group setting about something going on in your home, you never know who may secretly take advantage of the situation. You may have been telling mostly good things thus far about your husband but while you were doing that, the other person may have built a desire towards him for his good qualities. The moment you disclose some current challenges, that same woman may move in on him and that will open up a whole new set of possible challenges for your marriage.

I remember in the first 5 to 7 years of my marriage, my wife and I had many challenges. I wasn't used to some of the challenges we were experiencing and I felt like I didn't have too many people to talk to. I got married at 26 years old, so most of my friends were still single at that time. I didn't go to them because I felt like they wouldn't understand or could help me. That left me with only being able to go to my parents and that was one of the worst things I could have ever done. Here's the funny thing, my younger brother got married within a year or two of me and he did the same thing.

My brother, Zachary King says, *"What I've learned in the course of the relationships that I had is that you get a chance to create relationships in other people's eyes whatever way you want. I've learned if you speak and continuously have a certain type of conversation about the person that you're with, the people around you will start feeling whatever way you're actually feeling. So, in reality, it's really up to you whatever way you create the relationship of your spouse in speaking with friends or family. You will reap that reward or consequence down the line. So if you're not pleased with the way people around you see the person that you're with, I think you have to ask [yourself] how effectively you are communicating. When I think about my relationship with my ex-wife there was a lot of things that I did not know and so it's natural to turn to your friends and your family and try to get an idea or say, "is this normal? Is it normal that this happens or is it normal that that happens?" And so the percentage that I revealed to my family was a lot higher than the percentage I revealed to my friends. I think I revealed more to my family and I was more open about it because I felt like that was the reference that I had and I felt more secure about that. But the messages that I was giving to my family was a shock to my family because I had always laid out exactly how I wanted my marriage to be in practicing my way of life, and in practicing my religion. And so when changes happened and I started showing more ambivalence which was due to the relationship, it was very hard for the people around me. People don't handle change well. I think that inevitably you can create a monster that you are going to have to deal with because if you stay with the spouse you'll find that the company around you may not be all about your relationship as you are.*

The biggest piece of advice from what my younger brother is saying is that you have to keep in mind what you may be creating in the minds of your family when you speak about your spouse. My mother and wife did not get along for a few years because of the things I told my parents about my marriage, however, my dad didn't have an opinion one way or the other. Looking back now, I think he knew that marriages have their challenges, so he didn't get attached to the words I was saying about my wife. But my mom's thoughts about my wife were a reflection of the monster I'd created. When things got better in my marriage, my mom didn't adapt as quickly, so it caused some years of bad blood between the two of them. Needless to say, all is well now, but if I had known the possibility of the monster I was creating, I wouldn't have exposed my marriage to my parents at all.

The same concept goes for your friends according to Rod Shipman: "*I think it's important for you to always have someone that you can go to for guidance... what I've learned over the past several years is that you really need to limit how many people you actually let know your business because things can change at any given notice... I mean you can hate this woman this week because she made you go to the grocery store and she told you she doesn't want you going out with your boys or whatever. Then you go and gripe to all your boys and say, "she makes me sick, I can't stand her..." and then the very next week she goes to the store, fixes you a nice dinner and lays everything out for you and you two have a romantic evening and now your boys [have] this image of your woman just being this witch. Now you've got to come back and say she is this grateful person and you just love her and try to play damage control...So as a whole you have to limit what you say.*

For those of you who are still friends with people who have been there for you since day one or even some of your more recent friends that you've acquired, the same principle that applied for communication about my marriage with my parents applies for my friends as well. Every blue moon, you can find someone who won't judge you or who can be neutral. But the majority of your friends are going to form a negative opinion the more you expose the challenges of your marriage. And just like my mom, when things turn for the better, your friends may have ill feelings toward your spouse.

If you feel you have to share some information, get some advice or have a person as a sounding board, I suggest hiring a Licensed Therapist. Licensed Therapists are trained to be an unbiased party to help you navigate through the challenges of your relationship. Initially, you may feel the need to confide in your spiritual advisor and that is perfectly fine, too.. Be sure this person has a track record of being trustworthy, unbiased and has the fruit of a healthy, synergistic relationship that you admire. It would be great if wives could reach out to her maid of honor and the husband could reach out to his best man. Single and Engaged Ladies, whoever you choose to stand beside you at your wedding as your Maid of Honor and Best Man, these two individuals should be your first line of defense. That is why it is vitally important that you are intentional about who you choose to stand at the altar with you as you exchange wedding vows. Those two individuals have the responsibility to help coach, develop, nurture, and assist in keeping the marriage on track. Choose your Maid of Honor and Best Man carefully and intentionally. Although your impulse may be to choose someone that may be your "bestie", can she handle the assignment of protecting your marriage from divorce? Is your best man equipped with the wisdom and fortitude to hold the husband accountable to his responsibility as a husband? Your bestie may not be the best counselor for your relationship. They may not be able to bounce back when the road gets tough in your marriage. You must choose someone with wisdom, spirituality, neutrality, maturity, and someone who you know has love for both of you and who will fight alongside you to help keep you two together forever.

Empowerment Tools:

- Ideally, you should not tell anyone your business concerning your marriage
- Before you decide to expose your marriage to a third party, remember the possible consequences of:
    - someone telling your business
    - someone capitalizing on your spouse's weaknesses or yours
    - tension among friends and family
- Choose your counsel wisely:
    - Licensed Therapist
    - Spiritual Advisor
    - Maid of Honor/Best Man

...no man wants to stand in the room with other men who have been with his woman.

CHAPTER 7

Sex 101: What You Need To Know

IT WAS THREE days before my 16th birthday and I'd been "messing around" with this young lady. We went to a friend's house and I said to her, "My birthday is in three days. I want you to be my birthday present." A few moments later, it was all over and I was no longer a virgin. I remember being very happy because I was the last of all my friends to lose my virginity.

And then one day we grew up and we became fathers of daughters. You start to think about all the manipulative ways we used to have sex with women. Men think of daughters as a blessing and a curse. We think a daughter is a blessing for obvious reasons as she is our child, but the curse is that we may get paid back for all the things we did to women over the years. To combat what I felt would be karma when it came to my oldest daughter, I made sure very early on, I was very transparent with her about how guys think when it comes to sex. When she was eleven or twelve years old, I started telling her about the games guys play and the things they will say to get you to have sex with them. As a pre-teen she was saying things like "Dad, guys don't really think like you used to. You were just a hoe in school." But as the years went by and even up until today, she now says, "Yeah, Dad, I see what you're saying".

Most men will tell their daughters and close female friends that she should remain a virgin and guys like me knew that growing up so we'd set certain traps, have certain conversations, and run "game" on women. One of the things we know is although young girls are taught to wait, many of them don't know how to wait. There are certain techniques that men will use to trick women into having sex with them. This chapter discusses techniques that women need to understand about how men think about sex.

Trey Barnette: *I would say they need to watch out for "the game". The guy that has that confidence and has that game, really attracts all types of females. When a man has the look and the game, on average he's going to talk the panties off a lot of women…so I would tell my daughter to be careful of what these guys are saying and what they do ... the guys that come off ultra-confident to these women, they get "wow'd".... Then once the panties come off, it's a wrap. Let me say this, if your daughter is getting good sex, she's definitely going to be locked in to the man... so you definitely want to get her to the point where she doesn't fall for that. Some of the traps to look out for: anything that's risky against what Daddy would want, sneaking out of your house "Hey, come over here and kick it with me…I'm having a party...My parents are gone let's go upstairs to the bedroom...have a little drink...a little drink is not going to hurt you"…and the things that make a girl feel good and get attention... and I always say that girls want to have fun and girls want to have attention. If you can give them those two things, you can really trap them into anything...so a guy that has an open and fun-loving environment for a girl, they can trap them into anything.*

Rod Shipman: *Number one, you should never be at his house alone with him because there's no reason for you to be at his house at 14, 15, or 16 alone. My friends, back in the day, were running trains and girls say things like "all we want to do is come over and just watch TV", and the next thing you know, you're back in the bedroom... so if he asked you to come over to his house or can you come over to your house and your parents are not home, you should not be at home by yourself. Number two, if he comes at you with the whole "sex thing" saying things like "Let me just put the head in", you have to already know that he's out for one thing. If you've already expressed to him that you're saving yourself until marriage and he comes at you with that, then it's time to cut him loose because he's trying to do one thing and one thing only. Most guys if they're coming at you and trying to do that, they are only after one thing. A guy that's respectful is not going to come at you like that.*

Ryan Green: *In college, I was a songwriter and I was in a singing group. What I used to do was used my strength and what appealed to women. It was words and it was my voice. If I wrote a woman a poem or if I wrote a song for a woman I probably would "get it"... I was a chameleon and I'm not saying it as a braggadocios type thing but at the end of the day I paid attention to what women said and then I would become that... Woman need to pay attention to what they say because a man will switch to what they say just to get with her... if you're going to talk, I'm going to sit there and listen... For example, if she told me that she doesn't like something or she told me that she doesn't have a good relationship with her father, the next thing you know, I'm going to go be those things. It's not that I have malicious intentions at the time when I was doing it, but I saw that as just being a part of the game...and when I look back at it now that I'm older, it was pretty manipulative, but that's not where I was coming from... I thought I was just trying to be a good dude. I thought I was trying to be helpful and nice and be what a woman wanted. But really it was manipulative because I knew I wasn't trying to be in a relationship with them I was just trying to get a means to an end.*

Brian Clarke: *My approach was patience and constantly giving little flirts along the way and never ever pressuring them... I wouldn't even pressure her for a kiss. 90% of the first kisses were initiated by the woman for me and that's because I had a conveyor belt and there were always five to seven women and all of them were in different phases of the game... so I could take four months with you and barely hold your hand because I knew after I dropped you off, the person who I've been doing this [with] for months/year was already wide open. I was able to take my time and have patience and the cool thing about the body is flesh is reactive to touch, to suggestion, and your natural body craves sex...and it's your willpower that makes you stop...but it's your natural craving that's going to be sex so if you're just sitting down and I'm just talking to you and I haven't touched you in two months but you know I'm attracted to you and I want you, you're sitting at dinner wet and I don't even have to do anything...all I have to do is give you a kiss and a hug and you're going to say, "Oh, my gosh" and you will drive yourself crazy... and now in your mind it becomes a competition, "I'm going to make him want me" and honestly I do want you, I'm just being patient... so if ladies pay attention, a man's patience is game... I have more tips but I'm still using some of those on my wife so I don't want to give those away...lol*

Sam Smith: *The way that I approached everyone that I pursued was not with a thought process that you need to watch out for... My Approach was about finding time and finding something that they wanted to do. I wasn't one of those cats that had "game." My approach was more of listening and understanding and more importantly showing up as a gentleman. So it was the same for me whether my goal was to get to know somebody and date, or it was just sex, it wasn't a different approach for any of the women....I always try to kill them with kindness and there's really no "watch out" for that in my opinion. I would assume that if you're overly kind, then maybe you have a hidden agenda. But on the contrary if you're just showing up and you're just being respectful for me it was just being [an] Alabama boy with some Southern Charm.*

You can't really watch out for that because there is/was nothing wrong with being kind... but you may need to watch out for someone being overly kind as they may have a hidden agenda.

Rassan Austin: *You can't really coach women to have a strong male figure in their life because some of them are in situations whereas their fathers are not in their life, but if I had a daughter I would have such a strong presence in her life emotionally, physically, and mentally to where she understands how valuable she is and she doesn't need a man for anything. She doesn't need a man to find love because she can love herself.... she doesn't need for a man to show her attention or any of that and if she were looking for that then she could always find that with her dad. For the women who do not have a father figure in their life, I would say that they definitely want to seek a strong sense of self...you don't need to have sex to validate anything about you… you don't need to have sex to validate somebody's feelings for you or your feelings for them and I don't really know how to coach to gain a strong sense of self for a woman but I would say you want to be able to have that level of willpower to say, "No, I'm not ready to do this."*

One of the most interesting things about this topic is most of the fathers are hypocrites. We didn't hold on to our virginity, but we are the first ones to try and safeguard our daughters against having sex before marriage. As a matter of fact, out of the twenty-four men interviewed, only one of them was a virgin before marriage. Besides the morality that we've been taught to remain a virgin, one of the biggest reasons we try to protect our daughter's virginity is summed up in the words of Porter Bingham. He has two daughters and he said, "*One thing about our daughters having sex when it comes to most guys, you don't want to think of your daughter or have visions of your daughter getting humped by some dude.*"

We have some men who are amazing fathers and who take a more liberal approach to this topic.

Rafiq Shukur: *My daughter is 23 years old and I think that if you could sit her down and talk to her she would tell you what I did...Women are the safe guarders of sex and again it goes back to the fundamental rules and man's role as he's the hunter, but the woman controls everything about sex... unless you're talking about something unnatural or forced... The woman safeguards sex... when it happens and how it happens and that's a part of her role... so I said to my daughter that it would be best if she waited till she got married, but I'm also a realist and my counsel to her was that she needs to be very discerning about who she gives her body to...it's a gift and it's not one that you want to give away freely...men know when that gift has been given freely and women might say, "men don't know, they just care about getting theirs"... again that goes back to whether or not you're talking to a boy or man... men know when the goods have been given freely.*

Rodney Lawson: *What I told my daughter is to make sure that she understands the man's values... a man's values are surrounded by their beliefs and that leads to their actions... and they flow in a straight line and if you learn what a man's values are then you'll know exactly if he cares about you, you know exactly if he's willing to sacrifice for you and if you come across a man like that and you want to give yourself to him then by all means do it... I told her sex feels good... so guess what? I'm not going to tell you not to do it, but make sure you protect yourself... protect your feelings... make sure it's someone that feels about you the same way you feel about them... that's the advice that I gave her. I didn't tell her to not be a virgin or to hold onto it...I told her I know you're going to do it and I could tell you all day not to, but I know you're going to because the world functions that way and that's how society operates... what I wanted to do was educate her and protect...have her protect herself mentally and make sure it's not a man that is going to hit it and quit it... that's what was important to me... to instill the value in her [of]understanding a man before she gave it up... not to just give it up, but understand the man, before you make the decision to give it up.*

John Telley Gilliard: ...*One day I was watching a religious movie where this guy had a great relationship with his daughter and he told her, "I understand that I'm the man in your life that you measure everything against and he gave her this charm for a necklace and all I would like for you to do is that when you feel that you are ready to have sex when you feel like someone has earned the right for them to replace me as the man in your life come talk to me and give me the charm back and then we can talk because more so I don't want it to be just a feeling I want it to be more of a conscious decision of this is something that you want to do, this is the way that they make you feel and if you feel that this person will be there for you five or ten years down the road then by all means go for it. I would prefer for you to be a virgin, but I'll understand." As long as I'm putting the right things into my daughters they're actually going to make the right decision for themselves and that's all that any parent could ever ask for so I can't live their lives for them... all that I'm asking is that hopefully I've done a good enough job and then putting and sharing wisdom and stories and how much your worth really is...not just anyone can come along and have you, you're not just a piece of ass, you don't have to give up the ass just to get a bill paid, you don't have to have sex if you don't want to and you need to understand that you are in control and when someone comes along and they make you feel a certain way and you can see a future with them then by all means I'm not here to tell you not to do it because I didn't wait.*

None of these men are actually telling their daughters to go out and have sex. What they're saying is that you need to be smarter when making the decision should you choose to have sex. Although I have very conservative views regarding this topic, I believe John gave a great example of the father with the charm necklace from the movie. We are bombarded with sex via television, social media, and advertisements. We have the ability to access sexual content over the internet very easily but I think it's important to provide the necessary information to consider should you choose to remain a virgin or engage in casual sex.

Earlier I gave the example of what I said to the young lady in order to get her to have sex with me for my birthday, but I didn't tell you that the condom broke. I spent the next 30-plus days praying that she wasn't pregnant. My birthday is at the end of November, so needless to say, that was one of the worst holiday seasons as I sat worrying every day if she was pregnant or not. I remember how happy I was when her cycle showed up. I am sharing this because should a woman choose to have sex with a man, not only are there diseases and pregnancy possibilities, but there is also a thought process that men have about you. As you are making the decision to have sex or not, I want you to understand the thoughts of what the following men said regarding the question, "**What do men think about women who they can sleep with versus the women who are virtuous?**

Ryan Greene: *I'm not going to sit here and say that sex doesn't feel good because it does feel good but it's so much more to it than having a couple of strokes and bust a nut there's a spiritual exchange that takes place, there's an emotional exchange that takes place and there's all the stuff that happens that you don't even see when you're engaging in sex with someone... For men, it's easy for us because we're just giving whereas we're depositing into a woman... but a woman has to receive all that and she's in a vulnerable position because she's allowing someone into her body so when you do that you can't just do that and it not be a big deal and not come with consequences...what I tell my kids... they need to wait, try to wait...I'm not saying you have to be a virgin when you get married but you have to wait as long as possible because you just don't need that stress at a young age in school and you don't need that ...any problem relationship-wise can be solved by holding out if a girl doesn't know how a man feels about her.... just don't have sex with him... if he's still there then he likes you, if he still trying to pressure you every time, he may still like you but he's really thinking about himself more because he's trying to pressure you.... and let's not forget how God feels about having sex before you are married.*

Brian Clarke: *One thing that my pastor always says which really resonated with me... for every man that is trying to get at women just for sex, or even being in an unmarried sexual relationship, you're robbing that woman's future husband of that oneness of [being] first and you're sowing the seed on that and the reason why is because you have sex with her and you are now connected to that woman and now you're also in some way connected yourself to that woman's future husband so what I want to teach my daughter is do not rob your future husband of being the first one to be intimate with you... don't rob them of that, that is one of the biggest gifts you can give your future husband, that he's the first... and I will tell the boys don't rob that woman's husband of "firstness".*

Both of the gentleman are discussing a consequence far beyond the norm of disease or pregnancy. They are talking about the connection that occurs when you have sex with someone. As Ryan said, it's easy for men to have sex with women as they are making a deposit, but women are receivers of that deposit. Long after the man is gone, they are still holding on to that deposit. There are also animalistic qualities that men possess, whereas, we can make that deposit and move on to the next person with little emotional attachment. Other than being a prostitute or promiscuous woman, it may be difficult for most woman to receive the spirit of a man and then move on without some kind of spiritual or emotional attachment. To Brian's point, I challenge the women that want to get married one day to ask themselves this question before they give up their virginity or have casual sex, **"Do I want to rob my future husband of my body for this moment? Is this guy I'm about to have sex with worth it?"**

John Telley Gilliard: *There is a certain respect level for the women that you can't sleep with...I mean what is it going to take or is it just going to take a little bit more time...maybe I just haven't said or done the right thing. I have a buddy of mine that says "all women are like locks and every lock has a combination I just haven't put the right combination together"... and the women who we can sleep with, sometimes, there is a certain level of disrespect because if I can sleep with them I know this joker over here can sleep with them, so really they might not have any self-worth for themselves if that's all that they see themselves as....it's not that I don't have respect for all of the women that I slept with but I'd say maybe about half of them I have respect for because to be honest I meet you in the club and we go home I don't even* *know you but I'm beating it... and I know that I'm not the only joker that you probably did that to this week so really why are you here? You got the same thing I wanted, a nut... so that does diminish the respect but the women that kind of make you work for, it you have to wait a couple weeks, couple of months, couple dates, you say, "okay, this person sees herself as having self-worth and if I want to be around them I have to respect them... I can't just pick up the phone and call this person over and say, "hey, we f****** tonight? It's more of, "hey, I would like to see you... let's go see a movie, let's go to a ballet..."...or anything that exposes them to different things... if I find myself putting more effort into things that I think we can do then obviously I'm thinking of them as a person and I respect their time which means I respect them as a person as well.*

I want to acknowledge that I know it's difficult to just say, "**NO SEX FOR WOMEN UNTIL MARRIAGE**", however, if you are going to have sex, I encourage you to follow the directions discussed in Chapter 4...are you dealing with a boy or a man? That will at least give you a chance to determine if he is worth giving your body to. Oftentimes, women have a timeframe of two weeks, three months, six months, or one year to give a guy her attention and then they have sex with him. Previously, John alluded to giving us a chance to "unlock your combination", therefore having a little more respect for you. Conversely, you need to understand that if we can sleep with you very quickly, we have a tendency to have a lack of respect for you.

Rod Shipman: *...I respect women more because she's not going to give it up and she stuck to her guns, but not necessarily because some women that I might have slept with them once or twice and I respect them just as much as the person that did not give it to me and that's because women having sex can still have standards. I mean, yes, they gave it to me, but I don't [have] any more value for the ones that didn't give it up then for the ones that did. I know one woman who had only slept with one man in her life and I respected her... I still got the draws, but I respected her and I said to myself you know I appreciate you breaking a brother off... I mean it took me a minute to get it, but I got it, and I didn't think anything else about her.... I don't think I called her afterward either... lol*

So it sounds like a catch-22...if you quickly sleep with us, we probably won't respect you, however, if you make us wait to have sex, you still run the risk of being left behind. Keep in mind, all of this is occurring **before marriage.** But these are the risks of having sex before marriage that you should consider. This is the part of ***Sex 101*** you really need to think about.

Trey Barnette*: I think that for a man it's about getting to a level of accomplishment sexually. So when a man feels like he's conquered enough women, the ones that would easily lay down to him are boring. He might get with you if he's just bored and he doesn't have anything else to do... but I think the virtuous ones, and the ones that are a little bit of a chase... after a man has accomplished a lot of booty, virtuous women are more of an enticement.*

Rafiq Shakur: Y*ou have to go back to how a woman was raised. A girl that was easy to "get" was a girl I was not trying to have any parts [of] in particular because to me that didn't look like a model that I was familiar with. I was always more about the girl that made me wait or she wanted to build a relationship or if anything she was testing me to see if I was worth giving it up to. I would say it is very easy in this hyper-sex driven society to say that a virtuous woman loses out and you got to "give it up"...I would say it depends on whether you have short-term vision or long-term vision. The woman that is being virtuous is the one that's going to win, she's going to be popular, she's going to be dated in the short-term...and I would say that eventually one day a boy is going to grow into manhood and eventually he's going to want to settle down and he's going to mature and when he hits that point he's not looking at the chick that's giving it up... he's trying to find a woman that's not giving it up. So the message that society gives to a woman that you have to acquiesce to the strip club version of the woman or to the video vixen version of a woman or ladies you have to be the hunter... when the reality is if you have short-term goals and you can't think long-term then yes, you have to acquiesce...but you can bet your money that eventually boys transition into manhood and the type of woman that's attractive only a fool is going to marry the stripper, and I hope he can turn the hoe into a housewife... what becomes the sought-after woman is, "The Virtuous Woman" in the long-term so you can't give it up early and say, "I'm going to acquiesce to this foolishness" because when the time comes you're the one that's not going to get chosen.*

In the end, the virtuous woman...the one with standards, the one who can balance her feminine energy...that's the type of woman a man wants. Realistically, we would like the woman with experience, but let me tell you something that I learned long ago, no man wants to stand in the room with other men who have been with his woman. Ladies, hold on to your virtuous nature for as long as you can. It's what men really want.

Empowerment Tools:

- Understand the thought process of a man whether you have premarital sex or choose to hold onto your virginity
- The Virtuous Woman- the woman with standards, is more attractive to men in the long-run

I want to stand on top of a mountain and spread the message across the world of how painful it is to deny your husband sex.

Chapter 8

Sexual Rejection And How We Really See Intimacy

Allow me to transition your mind to one of the most important responsibilities of being a wife. Some might not understand the importance of how men view sex as being a vital function of an intentional wife. Before we understand how men feel when they are rejected by their wives, allow me to share the thought process many single men have as it relates to sexual rejection.

Raasan Austin: *As a man that's not married I don't have to deal with rejection because if you reject me that gives me access and the green light to go have sex with somebody else. If you are not going to give it to me I have options and its ok it won't become a point of contention I'm not going to fight you about it, it's cool, it's yours, I'm going to go get somebody else's.*

What Raasan just said sums up our thought process when we are single. What I notice from my research is that most sexually active single men think like this. But here's the interesting part, women know we think like this too. Other than for religious reasons, single, sexually active men rarely experience being denied sex from a woman when she starts having sex with him. As we mature, we think about settling down and being with one woman. During that time, most women are doing all they can in the bedroom to keep that man interested in her and wanting to proceed with marrying her. Then, they get engaged and in most cases, the woman is still sexually satisfying the man. At this point he is most likely getting maximum output from his woman. I have never heard a man that was engaged say, "we had to call off the wedding because she stopped having sex with me". Why is that? Because that woman is doing all she can to get him to the altar and she is not going to lose him by denying him sex. Most women feel that sexing his brains out is the nail in the coffin to keeping him interested in her and she also knows that denying him sex at this point will make it a competition for her against other women who may want him. At this point she is going to give him all the sex he wants, swing from the ceiling, and be as freaky in the bedroom as possible to keep his mind fixed on her.

Oftentimes, after a sexually active woman gets married, her mindset has the tendency to shift. She's "got him" now. Some wives become comfortable and there is less of a drive to continue to sexually engage her husband which is a fatal flaw for many wives. Let me ask a question: if I were to ask your husband if you guys have more sex now versus when you were dating, what would his answer be? Barring any health-related reasons, if the answer is, "no", then that most likely means that you could be denying your husband the quantity and perhaps the quality of sex he may desire.

Let's go deeper into what your man may be thinking. While you guys were dating he received all of the sex he ever could have wanted from you. Now that you are married and you are his only sexual resource you reject him? Now that the responsibility of supplying sex to him is a part of the covenant between the two of you, rejection becomes a part of your marriage on a daily basis? What's a man to do?

Let me share with you how some men feel when they are denied sex by their wives:

Charles Butler: *It makes you feel alienated. It makes you feel isolated. It makes you feel unloved. It makes you feel, depending upon how long it's been going on that you might have made a bad choice. I mean think about it, men...don't want to get married because they look at it like this, "Why would I put all my eggs into a basket that can eventually reject me? I'm taking care of you. I'm committed to you and just you... but in me committing to you now I have to suffer? I'm out here in these streets and I can have two or three or four on deck that if one doesn't want it then I can have this other one..." Men view it as, "When I wasn't married, I was getting more when I wasn't married then I am now that we can freely just do it." A lot of men view it as the ultimate slap in the face. I was telling a woman this one time and she said, "What if I don't feel like it?" and I said, "Okay, take that same view from everything that you need. If he walked in the house and didn't say nothing to you... walked right past you...didn't hug you, didn't tell you he loves you for a whole day... may have said a few words to you while grabbing something to eat... went upstairs, got in the bed, and he on Netflix on his iPad not paying no attention to you... and you're sitting there looking at him like, "are you going to talk to me? You didn't even hug me. You walked in the door, didn't say hello or ask me how my day was...." Wouldn't you hate that?" She said, "Yes." I said, "Why?" She said, "Because that's something that I need in a relationship." I said, "Oh, so you feel like you can just get what you need, but when it comes down to the sex and certain things that we need you feel like you can just pick that up when you want to like a buffet?"... You can't do that. It doesn't work like that.*

Ryan C Greene: *I wish that every woman could understand and see what it feels like to have that rejection. It's not to say that a married woman owes sex to her husband every single time he asks, but I think that each partner owes intimacy to their spouse... and your sex quotient should be discussed before you even get married... you both should know what your intimacy quotient is and be able to provide that to one another... Women will casually be like "not tonight" and they don't understand how that rejection affects us...women expect men to just get over it. Most of the time women process sex differently... they need the whole day of foreplay, the house cleaned, they need all these things out of their mind before they can have sex and men are like, "I'm here I'm ready now"... I try to stress to my wife and to any married couple, that when you get married you make a commitment that you are going to be the absolute only physical source of pleasure for your spouse and that is a huge responsibility. If you have plans that you are the only one that he's allowed to get sex from for the rest of your life, you have to understand that responsibility and be willing to sacrifice for that. Whether you look at it as a responsibility or a role, that's the role that you chose and that's the role that you have accepted in each other's life that you are the only source of physical affection to a married man.... it's not like he can go to work and say, "hey, I just really need a hug can you hold me" and just ask any woman just to hold him... you can't even go get hugs from anybody else but your wife...lol... so the wife has to understand that level of intimacy that's necessary and be willing to be that and that rejection is real and men deal with it differently but a lot of times it's so easy for them to say, "not tonight" and then you look up and then it'll be a week later and he'll be like, "Yo, what's going on?"... I ask men all the time, "When was the last time your wife actually approached you about sex versus you being the one that approached her?"... Just you even initiating sex as a wife will go a long way versus the man always having to be the one that's asking for the sex... I don't know how many husbands say, "No, Baby not tonight"...lol*

Zachary King: *I think this is an area that even though a lot of things have shifted in my life I think that's the one thing that's extremely damaging and there's a lot that could be said about this and it doesn't take a lot for me to say that a man in a lot of ways is a lot weaker than a woman in certain areas. I'm saying all that to say you have two people in a relationship that are impacted differently by what goes on and in this particular area the need for this physical connection is received very different for a man [than] by a woman sometimes. I think that there's enough evidence to say that it's received differently for a male vs female. A man could have a terrible day and the first thing that he wants to do is get laid. He doesn't want to come home and say, "Well, you know honey..." and then spend 2 hours talking about it... and I'm not saying that he won't do that but 9 times out of 10 the talking will happen after the sex... so there's some way that actually translates differently for a man versus a woman and unfortunately it's overlooked. The fact that a woman needs to say that a man needs to even earn it and it's an understanding that a man will be willing or trying to earn it indicates that a man is different in that way. When has someone said "I want my wife to earn having sex with me?"... so that already shows that men and women are different in how they value sex and it's an understood thing that we see it differently because otherwise we'd be making women earn it and obviously that is a joke... like go to work and say I'm going to make my wife earn it and watch how women will start laughing ....and why is that? Because something is different about how we experience sex. So with that said for someone who has experienced rejection before it is not taken lightly and that happening over and over again can be very destructive to your whole manhood.*

Brian Clarke: *I think that with anybody rejection is not good especially when it's coming from your spouse. That's the one place that God has given you as a safe haven where your body is not your own. Now it does depend on why there has been a denial or rejection versus "I'm just tired right now" or things are going on or that time of the month or you and your wife are just not feeling the best…Men can take that as rejection even though it was not rejection. Now if you're rejected because you didn't do something to your spouse's satisfaction, now you're compounding and you're truly outside of the garden of where God has intended for married life to be. So in general rejection is bad. [From] your coworker or your boss or friends... rejection doesn't feel good but it feels even worse coming from your spouse. I've been through it with my ex... there was a time that I didn't touch her for 5 months because...rejection had run so deep and so consistent because it was so many other things happening in the marriage that all the underlying schisms and resentments built up... and that's why you need to be very careful on how you reject your spouse…."hey, I'm not feeling the best so I'm not in a good mood but I'll get you later"... you should be open to have those types of conversations so you don't get rejected... so it goes back to having good communication between spouses and having the ability to express how you're feeling and what's going on in your life and your day... those conversations lead to closer intimacy... and it doesn't have to be sexual intimacy because sexual intimacy is the cherry on top to the intimacy that God wants you to have in your marriage. The intimacy and closeness and the love of God should be shown on each person. I'm directing God's love to my spouse and they should feel that... that is where the overall intimacy comes in whether it's the holding of hands, talking, the comfortableness, the expression of that love that He's given us as a gift is the sex part... so when you're rejecting your spouse, you're rejecting the gift that God has given us to have in that married life and you're not showing the love of God to your spouse here. He can't see God in you with a constant and consistent rejection.*

As you can see from these four men, rejection is not received well from your husband. I particularly chose these four men to speak on this topic, because all four of these gentlemen are divorced. Three of them are happily re-married. All of them experienced rejection in their previous marriages. One might argue the point of each of them having a thought process of needing sex so much as a reason why their marriage ended. So to the help you understand why rejection is such a difficult issue regardless if you are divorced or married, I want to share one of the major points from my Spiritual Advisor:

Chancey King says, "…it *buckles them at the knees. Even if they don't show it... the man could be the strongest manager or director or strongest leader in whatever capacity that they are in or preacher, you name it... but at home he becomes a cowering little boy in a corner that's hurting and doesn't even know what to do besides put on a facade when he walks out the door... and it breaks them down beyond who they are...*

Let's look at some of the words we've heard the men use to describe sexual rejection:

- hurt
- alienated
- isolated
- unloved
- confused

All of this leads to a key phrase from Chancey King where he said men "become buckled at the knees." I want to stand on top of a mountain and spread the message across the world of how painful it is to deny your husband sex.

Omar Finley: *I felt many times like what's the point? What's the point of everything we do? If we can't be intimate it's kind of like having the sweetest piece of candy sitting there but you can't eat it. It's a very depressing feeling... deeply depressing to the point where [we] become angry to some degree... it's a depressing, horrible feeling...I've always been able to get what I want and the problem for me is that I know how to get it. It's like there's all this gold out here and gold is good, but I got the diamond... but now I can't even enjoy the diamond... I can't even make it sparkle... and it makes you say, "Well, I might as well go get some gold"... that is the feeling that you get as if, "why am I wasting my time? Why am I playing?"...and to this day, I totally don't understand it.*

Ladies, there is a lot to be learned in what Omar said. Your husband has chosen you to be his wife. Part of that thought process is, "I used to get it from you and maybe even other women when I was single. I now feel that it is your responsibility to supply my sexual needs or very close to the same capacity that I received before I was married. If I can't get it from you, how long do you expect me to turn down other options?" Now, I'm not saying that statement is right, but I'm letting you know what he may be thinking and how your actions can fuel his actions to seek solace outside of your covenant. Can you expect your husband to continue to make the right decision to ignore other women if you are sending him out into the world each day lacking in the area that is your responsibility to fulfill?

I think the best analogy came from Charles Butler when he and I were on a panel of men for a women's conference. He said, *"If your man wakes up for work and before he leaves you cook him breakfast, there is a strong chance that he will not stop for breakfast on his way to work. If you prepared his lunch, when his co-workers come to him to offer a place to go to eat, he will most likely tell them No, he already brought his lunch. Around 3 p.m. he is going to get hungry, but if you call him and say he has steak and potatoes at home, when he drives home he is going to pass all those restaurants because he knows what he has waiting for him at home for dinner. So ladies do not send your man out of the door hungry because eventually, he is going to eat somewhere else."*

Now that we've established that sexually rejecting your husband is a problem let's look at a simple question: **Why aren't you having sex with him like you used to or at the level of his satisfaction? Is it health related? Are you sexually unsatisfied with his performance? What is going on?**

Donald Bell: *Whenever we talk about sex and the man isn't getting it when he wants to or the woman is not getting it when she wants it or it's not going down how either of them had hoped for it to be, there's a deeper issue... why are you rejecting your husband? What is it? What's going on? ...because it shouldn't be a constant, "Can I get some? Can I get some? Can I get some?" and then you're waiting for that, "yes" and that happens once a month... it shouldn't be that type of thing. Sex in a relationship is supposed to be free flowing... and yes sometimes even with my wife, we may schedule it because for example based upon our schedules we haven't seen each other in two days... so when I get home on Wednesday at 7 o'clock it's about to go down... that's one thing... but there's usually a deeper issue if the man is constantly getting rejected and the woman is constantly not wanting to be with her man, something is going on...*

If your husband has come to you expressing concern about the lack of sex or perhaps you may be feeling that you may not be sexually pleasing him, consider this situation, "mission critical". Take an active role in working with him to fix your sexual situation. If your home was on fire, you would not only work to find the source, but you would do all you could to make sure that fire was extinguished. Consider lack of sex or refusing to give him sex as an out of control fire that has to be dealt with immediately or it will burn out of control.

The men and I went on to discuss, **"how would you coach your daughter about sexually satisfying her husband?"** It was a consistent message of "as often as possible" from all the men on the panel. This included them saying, "have sex every day or one to two times per week." No one said, "don't worry about it"...lol...so I would venture to say that this topic is something that you have to deal with if you want to get married and stay married. If you don't think you can hold up this expectation, then do not get married. It's just that simple. Do not think that you can get married and you can change his mind about this topic. Don't listen to your friends about "training him" to do what you want. It's a lie. You are not training him to be less sexual. You are opening him up to resentment that may manifest in other ways. When you say, "I do," you are saying that you desire to be all he will ever need sexually. Things may change or you may not be in the mood sometimes, but when you decided to get married you also accepted the responsibility to maintain your role of meeting your husband's sexual needs.

Harold Brinkley: *I would say as much as his appetite allows... keeping that man happy... If you're in the ideal relationship whereas a man is handling his responsibilities and the woman is assuming the responsibilities of a woman, then she should be assuming the role of satisfying him sexually as often as possible...people came up with this phrase, "happy wife, happy life" but I don't necessarily believe in it... as a man who's the provider, you want that man to be a happy provider and she needs to go above and beyond to make sure he's taken care of and his kids are taken care of... if he's being the right provider or at least trying to be, you will get a lot more out of him if you make sure that he's happy in this area... his happiness turns into your happiness eventually... it's a trickle-down effect.*

The phrase, "Happy Wife, Happy Life" is one of the worst phrases ever coined. Why? Because happiness comes from so many different places, that it's impossible to totally fulfill the "Happy Wife" category. I've been married 14 years and the needle is always moving to what makes her happy. Women evolve and as they do, their "happy meter" moves. This means that the man will continuously chase doing what you want him to do to make you happy. If he's always chasing your happiness and your happiness isn't consistent, then at what point are you really happy? Your husband is the head in the marriage and if he is taken care of, you will be taken care of when he receives the proper nourishment. If you sexually satisfy your man, the benefits of his happiness will far outweigh the thought process of, "Happy Wife, Happy Life." His sexual satisfaction not only benefits you but the entire family in the long run.

Chancey King: *I would say as often as possible but within the context of reality. You cannot leave a man alone...keep in mind that when you're not real and just having sex for the sake of it, it doesn't benefit... so I would say to have sex as often as possible within the realms of reality because the intent of it amongst the two companions in the right relationship is supposed to fulfill all the physical needs that you have within each other and to shut out every aspect mentally, and psychological challenges that you're dealing with in life that is the blockage... sex helps to build each other up and helps you to come out into the next day knowing "I'm a better person because of you."*

There are two things I'd like you to keep in mind. If your man loves you, he understands what the "realms of reality" are. Let's assume that both you and your spouse have discussed each other's sexual appetite. It is important to note that unrealistic expectations need to be managed upfront or along the journey of marriage in order for both of you to be on the same page. Additionally, if you understand how important sex is to your husband and the benefits you will receive in the long run, then there should never be a time where you just do it for the sake of doing it to shut him up. If you are doing this, please stop. Your husband can feel it when you are going through the motions. A dead lay is almost worse than denying him. If you feel this is the case, it is your responsibility to communicate to him what would be more helpful to get you in the mood. Saying, "Not tonight, I'm not in the mood" is not acceptable, but perhaps, "I'm not in the mood but this is what you can do to help me get there". It shows your husband that you have acknowledged his needs, expressed your mood, and are now willing to collaborate with him on finding a solution. Perhaps you can explore ways that can help you rise to the occasion. It is not solely your husband's responsibility to turn you on. You must get creative and work together to find ways to fulfill his sexual needs.

If you are a virgin or celibate and you are unsure of your sexual quotient, it's okay. Maybe this will help:

Zachary King: *...that's a piece that needs to come in a conversation in the pre-marriage or when you're looking to become serious. One of the questions that I started asking after being married the first time, I wanted to know if the woman knew stuff about her body or do you know whether you're one of those types of people that need to have sex a lot and in your mind how much is that. It's just like a business. If we both have the same ice cream business, you might be pushing way more units than I do. So if I ask you a question, "Do you put out a lot of ice cream? and you said, "Yeah."... Now in my head I'm thinking a lot of ice cream might be five hundred cones in two hours and you're thinking a lot of business is 100 cones... but that's my bad in not being specific. So... being specific without being rude that needs to come out. I was talking to somebody who didn't have sex because she was a virgin so I was* *like, "What's the situation with you? Are you someone who feels like you really need to get married because you're trying to have kids or is it because you don't feel like you can hold it together and not have sex?"....Being somebody who has been a virgin before I got married, I also know that you don't know what it's like and you can't know certain levels of the desire until you actually have sex... I've always been more of the upfront person. Somebody needs to be responsible and have the conversation...*

I think this is important to mention because a virgin doesn't know what he/she doesn't know. I would encourage you to have the mature conversation of what you are thinking may be your expectation of sex upfront with the understanding that it is possible your husband may require more than what you may feel is necessary. Have the flexibility to work towards adapting to his needs. If it turns out that he doesn't have an expectation beyond your ability, great. Just as long as you are willing to step up to the challenge of meeting his sexual appetite is all that is required and that willingness will allow him to work with you to meet an expectation that both of you can benefit from.

I want to conclude with something that Charles Butler said. *"The shop always needs to be open. It needs to be like Waffle House, 24 hours a day, 7 days a week. I remember my ex-wife wrapped herself like she was a burrito in the sheets, and didn't talk to me for like 2 days... and it makes you feel like, "Why are we even together?" I mean it's like there's no point...we spent all this money...we had a wedding and we did all this stuff to get down to it just being about me and you and we don't know how to protect each other in the relationship. Giving what the person needs also protects them from outside sources...you don't want him to cheat and you don't want him to entertain any other stuff. You have to give folks what they need because they need it and because it protects you guys' relationship. If you are not having sex with me, you are not protecting me."*

Rejecting your husband as it relates to sex reduces the protection of your marriage on many levels. It opens up the propensity for him to engage in masturbation, pornography or perhaps even seeking solace in another woman. Having sex with your husband reinforces the bond between the two of you. It helps him think more clearly, reduce his stress, and many other health benefits of how sex positively impacts his overall well-being. It is your responsibility to assist in maximizing the protection of your marriage and ensuring your husband does not feel rejection as it relates to his sexual needs.

Empowerment Tools:

- Make sure your "before marriage" sexual performance is just as consistent after marriage
- Be mindful of each other's sexual appetite and do your best to be consistent
- Don't reject him with negative words but find alternative solutions to satisfy his needs
- Work together to achieve maximum intimacy and sexual satisfaction with your husband
- Protect your marriage from outside sources...he needs your body more than you realize

Double standards will always exist no matter what society tells you.

CHAPTER 9

Sexual Double Standards: Men Vs. Women

IN THE LAST two chapters, we've gone from discussing the importance of being a virgin and how men view a virtuous woman to discussing key factors for wives consider in order to maintain or improve their marriages. Before we get into the topic of discussion for this chapter I'd like to take you on a quick journey and share a quick story about my teenage son, Evian.

I went to see him in a play when he was in the 4th grade. When the play was over we were walking out of the theater and this lady dropped something on the ground. He immediately ran to it, picked it up and said, "Here you go, ma'am." She smiled and said, "Wow, you are such a gentleman." Over the years I've watched him open doors for ladies, pull chairs out for them, and he's even been on the train and offered his seat to a woman in order for her to sit down. Every time I witness his chivalry toward women, it makes me proud to see him perform some of the teachings we have shown him over the years when it comes to how to treat a lady. Whenever he does a courteous deed for a woman she will say, "Wow, chivalry isn't dead".

Most women prefer a man who is chivalrous. I mean who wouldn't like their chair pulled out, an umbrella held, a door opened, and the myriad of things that men do for women in being polite to them. I've always wondered something about chivalry. Why aren't women chivalrous to men? Why don't women pull out chairs for men? Why don't women give up their seats for men? Why don't men walk on the inside of the sidewalk when they are walking with a woman versus the outside?

If we look at society's statements regarding women being equal to men and how a woman can do everything a man can do, why hasn't the etiquette of chivalry adapted to the code of society? Now I think a very small amount of women would agree to change the rules of chivalry. Many women believe that men are supposed to do these things, but doesn't that seem like a double standard? I think it is. But there are many double standards that we live by every day, for example, chivalry.

What about the fact that women have a cycle and every month endure cramps? I hear that cramps are painful and can cause a woman to be irritated or emotional for a few days. Because of this social and biological norm, men must understand and be more sensitive to women during these times. I don't think it's fair that women get a reprieve every month because biologically their bodies are menstruating. Why can't men get a few days to be emotional every month? If men and women are equal, then women should be able to suck it up, fight through the pain, and not be emotional, right?

Now I'm sure you are wondering why I would say such a harsh and insensitive thing, but although it may sound harsh, it is a double standard that women are allowed to be more emotional at times. Generally speaking, men do not want to be labeled as misogynistic, patriarchal or chauvinists, but we do want to drive the point home that women use double standards to their advantage at times. I find it funny how stereotypes and labels are a problem when it comes to the workplace but when we begin to explore the emotional side of a woman and the pass women get to be emotional it just seems unfair and unrealistic to vacillate between the two notions.

What is my point here?

As I looked at this topic concerning double standards, I almost skipped this subject because some people may not be mature enough to handle how men think about it. But I felt it was necessary to include because I would like women to understand how men think about it. Women have evolved into thinking that because of the stereotypes and factual data of how men can have multiple sex partners that women can too. I thought this was a great topic to discuss with the men in order for you to read their thoughts on the double standard of men versus women when it comes to having multiple sex partners.

Rod and Harold shared what most women hear regarding the subject of having multiple sex partners.

Rod Shipman: *Yes, I do think it's nastier if a woman is having sex with multiple men, but either way it's still not right for us to feel that men can do it and women can't.*

Harold Brinkley: *It's pretty simple it's a double standard and it's not acceptable for a woman to sleep with multiple men.... no guy wants to be on the receiving end of being in a room and someone having the luxury of saying that they were with your woman. No guy wants to be at the end of that because men are petty... lol...*

If we are going to have this conversation, we have to start with the conservative, average view that men have on this topic. On average, men do not want to marry a woman who has been with a lot of men. One of the major reasons why is to Harold's point, we don't like the thought that some other men have done certain things to and/or with our woman. When he used the word "petty" I would substitute that with the word "ego." On average, our egos will not allow us to accept our life partner being a "hoe" prior to marrying her.

Ryan Greene: *Yes, it is a double standard that we want to go out here and do whatever we want to do. And we want our women to be virgins and the reason why is because we as men do women dirty. The women that we've been with, we've done sexually dirty things with them and we don't want our main chick to be one of those girls that was treated the way we've treated other women. You don't want any other man to be able to look at your girl and say, "yeah, I did this, this, and this with your wife or with your woman."... so it's an ego thing. We want to both be able to do it to all the women that we've had, but don't want our women to be one of those victims from another man.*

You can call it ego, selfish, whatever you want, but most men will never take kindly to a woman who is promiscuous. Some men feel this way because of the biological factors that come into play.

Trey Barnette: *Well, off the record and on the record if a woman had as many sex partners as me I would be questioning how was she still walking... lol... But if I was in a relationship with a woman and she had half the amount of sexual partners as me, then I would question her... and yes, that is a double standard and I think that it is in a way justified because of the overall sense of what a man and a woman are in a relationship...so our perspective of relationship or sex is different. For example, if a woman had 25 partners, was she really emotionally connected with all these guys? If she wasn't, then the question is, "Were you just being a slut?...*

and people can say it's a terrible double standard, but it is true... and I'll go get the anatomy and physiology real quick... so when it comes to sex it's really for reproduction and for us to go from Adam and Eve to hundreds of millions of people, men had to play an active role in reproducing with multiple partners. Men can reproduce every 45 minutes to 1 hour whereas women can only reproduce every 9 months... so our sexual organs just naturally drives us and it's set up for men to have more sex than women... so I'm not only breaking it down from the double standard and monogamy perspective but also from an anatomy perspective and if you look at it that way then you say a man is built to have more sexual partners than women.

Trey acknowledges the double standard but gives good reason and insight on how men view a woman who has had multiple partners. Here is a moment where a woman has to pick which "poison" they want. On one side, men know that a woman is going to have an emotional attachment to a man she is sleeping with. And if the woman says she has no attachment to multiple partners that is going to raise a red flag. As a man why would I want to be with the woman who sleeps around and has no emotional attachment? That does not seem natural to me. Women are wired to become emotionally attached when they have sex with a man. If she can turn those feelings off and on as she pleases, my thought process would be what else can she turn off if I happen to want to move forward and be in a committed relationship with her? That's not a street I want to go down, therefore, this lady would not be someone I will commit myself to.

On the other side, the lady is just sleeping around and like Trey said, she is viewed as a "slut." What good man wants to marry a slut even if he is a "hoe" in his own right? This ties back to Ryan's point that we don't want to imagine your past with that number of sexual partners.

Charles Butler said, *"Personally and morally it's wrong no matter what gender does it. The right way is one man, one woman in Holy Matrimony. And through this "free love" and "have sex with anybody you want" ideology, it destroys relationships as a whole. I think that if women think if they can do what a carnal man does, then it really sets them up to be in a situation where they continue to not get what they desire. These women are desiring marriage. They're desiring families. The more and more you paint this picture of "be with whoever you want, have sex with whoever you want", it keeps you in the mindset of not wanting to be in a relationship and not wanting to be married. You feel like, "I can get the things that I desire whenever I want from whomever I want and I won't have to commit to nobody,"... and I think that that's a really big problem in our society. Lastly, I just don't believe it is right on either side. One of the reasons why I feel like people may feel like one side gets away with it and the other side can't is because our sexual organs are on the outside. Everything that we do has to do with giving out and once we've given out it's kind of like, "Okay, we're good". But women are carriers and it's almost like when you picture a woman being with a whole bunch of men, you picture her carrying a whole bunch of men with her. You don't have that picture when you look at a man. You don't have the picture of "he's been with a lot of women, so he's carrying a lot of women with him." You think about it with a woman. If a woman says she slept with 30 guys, you're thinking she's carrying around 30 men with her..."*

If you ask my daughter or wife about my past, they will probably chuckle and say I slept with a fair amount of women. Neither one of them know the number of women I have been with and honestly, they don't care. Even if I told them it was 50, they would probably just say, "You were a hoe" and laugh and move on. But let's say hypothetically my son asked my wife and she said she slept with 50 men. I guarantee you he would never repeat it, there will be no chuckle, and he would probably get upset. Why is that? To Charles's point, although it is a double standard, the visual picture that you get in your mind of a woman with multiple partners is different. And just like chivalry, that picture will never change. So, Ladies, I caution you as you deal with this double standard, what do you want your possible mate to picture you as one day? Do you want him to look at you and realize your high body count as it relates to sexual partners?

I am not ignorant of the fact that there are some ladies who have had multiple sex partners or perhaps been married multiple times. Please do not feel like we are judging you because that is not the case at all. The goal is to help women understand how men think about women who engage in casual sex. If that is what you choose to do, enjoy yourself. My assignment is to simply be the messenger and properly prepare you to meet and marry the man of your dreams. Allow me to throw our experienced ladies a lifeline. There are some men who couldn't care less how many sexual partners you have had. As long as you can commit to him and love him, he will not allow it to be a hindrance in his fidelity to you. Take a look at a few more perspectives from our panel regarding this topic.

Delante Murphy: *I don't really care if a woman has slept with a lot of dudes because at the end of the day if that woman is not a virgin, it doesn't matter if she slept with one person before you or 400. She slept with somebody else before you so if it's a question of your safety and you feel concerned, then do your thing. But I can't judge anything behind them. I can only deal with the present with me and what I want and what I require... So if a woman is out there getting hers, and I know women like that who are professional but they sleep around and I'm ok with that as long as they are being safe.*

Kevin Gray: *I feel like that it is not fair but I do think that society has now shifted their views on men who cheat and have multiple partners. There is something wrong with that… I think that society is in the place now whereas it is very rare that you find a couple that is faithful and monogamous to one another…. but that is what people expect... and as soon as a man is found to not be faithful all hell breaks loose. In my younger years, a woman who has multiple sex partners... I did not approve and I still do not approve. However now that I'm more mature, I'm not going to look down on her any more than I would look down on the guy that's doing it.*

Rodney Lawson: *Society has made that rule and if women do it then they are looked upon as some type of cheap person and some type of cheap piece of meat... but I will say that's not the type of woman that I'm going to be with. It is difficult to give you a direct answer about that...if you are sleeping with a bunch of men like that, there's no intimacy and something is broken and it's really the same thing for a man.. Men do that because they take longer to mature. They can go well into their senior years before they finally get past that sometimes and some don't really mature... but I'm not sure if you realize it's not about how many you can get, but it's about that one that shows you the level of intimacy that you're not willing to mess up. I have always felt this way with anybody who I consider as marriage material... but if you're not marriage material you can sleep around as much as you want to and that's not going to bother me... if a woman wants to be marriage material, she needs to show respect for herself. If she is not showing respect for herself, then that's when she's going to sleep with a bunch of people. If she's sleeping with a bunch of people, it actually translates to something that is broken inside.... she feels like she has to sleep with a bunch of people to get validation.*

So there you have it, Ladies. Rodney said you can sleep around all you want and it won't bother "The Rodneys" of the world. On the contrary, you could eliminate or drastically reduce your chances of becoming a wife, but hey, good luck with that should you ever want a man to consider you his queen.

Rafiq Shakur: *Multiple sex partners does not bother me as much as a woman's attitude about having multiple sex partners. At this point in my life, it would be pretty miraculous to meet a woman who has not had multiple sex partners... but if she feels that her attitude is, "I can do what a man can do and therefore, I can have multiple sex partners" ... see now we're talking about two separate things. The attitude that a woman can do what a man can do is problematic... and it goes back to the distortion of roles and I would argue that people would say that it's a double standard. A man that feels he can have a bunch of sex partners, he's actually contorted in his role as well... so it's actually a double-edged sword and problematic on both ends. I do not think that it's okay for a woman to think that she can do what a man can do. That's a distortion of roles at its core and I say to her, "Yeah, you can do it, but there's going to be some problems that's going to come with that..."*

Ryan C Greene: *I feel like instead of women trying to be like men. Whether it's right or wrong, they should actually try to pull men in the opposite direction. As men get older, they're always getting bombarded with the message that that's how you prove your manhood. "Go out here and have sex with as many women as possible"... but as we get older, we start to realize how you might have been having fun, but that's not what being a man is really all about. There is so much more to it and instead of me trying to be out here and smash as many women as possible, maybe the men should be held to the same accountability as women versus women driving to sleep with whoever they want to like men. Tell the woman, "don't have sex" and he just won't have sex with them and then you won't have these problems... and then you say, "Well, men can have sex." Well, then you have to ask yourself a question: do you want to deal with all the issues that come with having sex like you think men do or do you want to live a more peaceful life? Who has not had sex and in the end the woman is pregnant? There's nobody who has not had sex and ended up paying child support. Or there's no one who did not have sex and ended up with an STD. There's nobody that has not had sex and then still have "Baby Mama Drama". One of these is going to happen. So instead of trying to be like men on that one, you need to look at the ultimate consequences that are waiting for you.*

As I conclude this chapter with the last two statements from Rafiq and Ryan, I'd like to bring your attention to the tone of what they shared with you. The message I want you to receive is that women need to stop trying to act like men and be women. Whether its sex or any other role, please stop trying to be a man. You will never be a man no differently than a man can be a woman. Double standards will always exist no matter what society tells you. Some of them you benefit from and others may be a challenge.

Being a woman represents strength, knowledge, wisdom, understanding, fortitude, courage, tenacity, adaptability, and a myriad of other positive qualities.

It's hard enough being a woman in today's society. Why would you want to make your life more difficult by trying to act like a man in any capacity? I encourage you to spend more time maximizing your role as a woman. As you master the art of femininity, you will tap into the secrets that many, "Baby Boomer" women apply to their marriages on a daily basis. Now, this is not to say that you have to be extreme in how you express yourself as a modern woman but there is a secret hidden in plain sight which is that a woman's role is far more powerful than a man's role when it is properly maximized. Ladies, I admonish you to spend your time maximizing being the woman you were created to be, and master the art of who you were created for--the man. If you truly embrace your femininity in its fullness, you will reap more benefits choosing the path of being a beautiful woman versus the path of thinking, being and acting like a man.

Empowerment Tools:

- The male ego cannot handle a woman who has had multiple sex partners void of emotional attachment. Rethink promiscuity, you are marriage material.
- Some men are perfectly fine with women having multiple sex partners, even though it is frowned upon, there are some men who would be happy to build a life with you so do not be discouraged.
- Maximize your femininity. Your role as a woman is so much stronger than that of a man.

You must understand that cheating is not the start, it is actually the beginning of the end.

CHAPTER 10

Why We Cheat

THERE IS A television show about a man who is married and he has met a woman who has become "the side chick". Although various parts of the show are exciting, the main plot is about the relationship between the married man and the side chick. I never really watch it too much because I try to stay away from shows that can get me hooked to the point where I am glued to the television at that particular place and time. One of the most interesting things I have witnessed with not only my own wife, but many other wives of friends of mine, is how many women became sympathetic to the relationship. The story line shows the man's interaction at home and how disrespectful the wife is to him along with the lack of sex, and other life events taking place in the home. Suddenly, the scene switches to the life of the side chick eventually showing her first encounter with the married man. And of course, they have sex. Sometimes he would even cry over her and she over him. I'd just sit there and watch my wife cry or I'd look on social media and see women saying, "Aww, she loves him" or "he would do anything for her, that's so sweet..." and I'm saying, "WAIT A MINUTE!!! So you are saying that the infidelity scenes are okay here?" And some women replied, "Well, look how his wife is treating him..." And I'd just shake my head. Not because there isn't truth to what they are saying but it's just interesting to hear it come out of a woman's mouth as if the interaction between the man and side chick are okay because of how the wife is treating the man at home.

There's no way I could write this manual without empowering you with tools for a lasting relationship by helping you understand the thought processes of why men cheat. A friend of mine said I am "dry snitching" or in other words, sharing the secrets of the male species and he is absolutely correct. According to my

"Street 101" dictionary, dry snitching is when you tell the truth about something and/or expose someone or group without saying the person or group's name directly. But I'm not really dry snitching, but more helping to bring an understanding. My assignment is to help you understand the thought process of a man when it comes to cheating. My panel and I are going to give you some things to think about to reduce or prevent his thoughts of cheating. I say thoughts, because that's how it all begins. Of the men who I know who have stepped out on their wives, none of them woke up one morning and said, "I'm going to cheat on my wife today" with no prior thought process behind it. Cheating begins in the mind. There are several reasons why a man cheats but my assignment is to point out how much a wife may contribute to her husband cheating.

Let me state for the record that I am not endorsing the actions of any man who has stepped out on his marriage nor am I attempting to blame women for the reason their husbands may have cheated on them. For those of you who are unmarried who have experienced "cheating" in your dating, monogamous relationship, he did not cheat on you. Was he unfaithful to your commitment? Yes. Was he well within his right as a single man to sleep with another unmarried person? Yes. Was it okay for him to lie to you and sneak around with another woman? No. I know that is a hard pill to swallow but there is no such thing as "cheating" or "infidelity" outside of the covenant of marriage. But for the married ladies, this chapter has been designed to share thoughts on why married men cheat and how to do all you can to "cheat-proof" your marriage.

Before we get to the panel's responses regarding infidelity, allow me to share some high level insight with you. As with most things that occur, there is a beginning and an end. When you run track, you have the start and finish line. If anything is made on this planet, you have a point where the item begins production and a point where it is finally ready to launch. Even when writing a book, you have the beginning and the conclusion. I can go on with many examples but ultimately you need to understand the concept of cheating and where it begins. If you desire to protect your relationship from infidelity, there are a few things that must be considered. You must understand that cheating is not the start, it is actually the beginning of the end. Most people get confused about this because you will hear a woman say, "We got a divorce because he cheated." And when I hear that, I say to myself, "Lady, you didn't get a divorce just because of that."

Cheating is normally not the problem. Cheating is a symptom of the problem. What do I mean by this? What if I walked up to you and struck up a conversation and two minutes later sneezed all over you? Imagine that sneeze was full of disgusting spit and yellow mucus right on your face. How would you feel? We can assume that if anyone was standing there, they would probably agree with you that I have a problem, right? However, what most people might not know is that I sneezed because I am allergic to pollen. The pollen in the room is the problem. No one can really see that part, they just see the sneeze. Although I could have covered my mouth, turned away, or grabbed a tissue before sneezing, I didn't. Now, the sneeze looks like the problem but if I had taken my medicine like my doctor told me to, there is a high probability that the sneeze would have never occurred. Cheating on your spouse should NEVER happen, but let's move beyond the symptom and look at the root cause on why someone has or may cheat in the future. Understanding the root cause(s), can help us prevent the problem from occurring or reoccurring in our marriages. The question posed to our panel was, **"Why do men cheat?"**

Delante Murphy: *I think there could be a lot of selfishness. Men are like babies. A lot of times when we're ready to have a woman or want the woman to be there, it's like we just want her there to fall in place at the right time and we get impatient... Imagine the Soviet Union Army, and they are in precision and walking... so it's kind of like how we look at a woman. When you do come to that line, get in line, and don't miss a beat... and if you don't make it, and you're not there, and I'm missing a gap in my formation, then it's like what the f*** is going on? I'm not married, but I've heard that most married men stop getting head from their wives after a while... but they did that to get you, but now you only giving him head on his birthday. So is he supposed to just wait one day per year to get head from his wife? And then when he ask you about it, you told him to get out your face, and then he's going to cheat because what he requires she's not doing. I'm just giving you that as an example of something because it's not about "head". It is in the lack of those various packages of a man's importance from his woman is what makes men cheat... and the thing is that men tell women that they're about to cheat, women just don't hear it. For example, if a man tells his wife he would like to have some head, and he tries to get you to do it, and you don't want to do it, and you like "nah. I'm cool. I'm tired." If it don't happen* *after a while, he's going to say "I really do like this. What's your problem?" and she says "I really feel blah, blah, blah"... and he'll say, "I really need this".... Now, he's not going to say I'm going to get with another chick. He's going to ask a few times as a request and it depends on his patience. Then eventually he's going to go get it from somewhere else... He could say, "I'm tired of you nagging me, can you lay off me for a minute" If she keeps nagging, he's going to seek something else. Then when we're out at the bar or we [are] at a lounge after work, and we [are] chilling, and he makes a comment, "my wife getting on my last nerves".... and then here comes her [reply], "I would never nag you. You a man. My job is to be your comfort when you get home and be your peace of mind"... and then you're like really? ...and then she like, "I'll suck your d*** every day"... and you're like, "Really? Even on Sunday?" and then she's like, "Even on Sunday..." and that's how he end up cheating.*

One of the funniest, most candid interviews I did was with Delante. Now, some of you may read this and be disgusted or think it's crass. If you read between the lines, he gave about 4 different points to pay attention to. But like most men, we don't always say the right things or we may not communicate how we feel in the manner we should. So the point gets lost in translation.

<u>Here are Delante's Key Points:</u>

1. A man may cheat if he feels neglect or lack from his wife
2. A man may cheat because he is selfish
3. A man may cheat if his wife does not perform the same sexual favors as she did before marriage
4. A man may send several messages before he cheats.

For those of you who may be lost already, let me give you the number one reason that came from 99% of the men interviewed. The major reason men cheat is that of the word "lack." Most of the men repeatedly used this word in discussing the major reasons for men cheating.

Charles Butler*: Two reasons: if a man is not getting what he needs. I think any man will be put in the position, and you can set your man up to cheat, who's not a cheater, by not giving him what he needs. It's actually the same way with a woman... cheating goes beyond a sexual experience. The cheating actually happened before you even got in the sack because you bonded* *with that person on an emotional level because you were lacking something in your covenant and in your relationship. I think that's one side... and I think the other side of the man, he's out of control sexually. He does not know in the age of strip clubs on every dark corner, and the accessibility of porn just one click away, it puts men in this fantasy world about sex, and they don't really respect it... and sometimes you could become an addict to it and not really know how to say no and control yourself. So you're talking about two different situations. If he's not getting what he needs, and you're rejecting him and you're denying him sex or you're raising hell and don't give him no respect, but you expect him to be loyal? That's a very demonic situation to be in. It's almost like I'm not going to feed you, I'm not going to be nice to you, I'm not going to be kind to you, I'm not going to give you what you need, but you better be back in this house and you better give me what I need... or because you didn't give me what I need, I'm not going to give you what you need. A lot of that stuff warrants the enemy... and like I said earlier you're not protecting your husband. If he's a good man...if he's been faithful to you, coming home to you, working hard... doing the best he can to be the best father he can... I mean he's not going to get it all right, but if you take care of that man and make him feel like a superhero, he is going to jump through rings of fire to make sure that you guys are okay... so I think it's twofold: is he a sexual addict or...just not getting what he needs as a man.*

Chris Jackson: *Ultimately, I think that men cheat because they're looking for a deeper level of connection that they're not receiving whether it is sexuality or femininity. I feel that most men like the energy that they get from cheating because there's an energy that we get from women... and there's a level of energy that we get from a woman who's at her highest feminine level of essence, and it feeds men... it's like an intoxicating perfume that just pulls the man in... so with that said, what do you think happens when you are being more masculine than feminine as a wife?...and meanwhile, there are women on your husband's job or out in public, that have their femininity turned all the way up... how long do you think he can resist that level of intoxication? To ignore or to dismiss a man, is giving him permission to cheat. You have to think about it. We are very simple creatures. And we have to remember those basic needs that we talked about earlier about sex, food, and encouragement... so if you don't take care of those basic level needs, then eventually he is going to cheat. And it's not that he's out there looking for it, but there's somebody out there, and they play, and they're sexy, and their fun, they cook, or whatever the case may be... and they do the things that you don't want to do? Do you expect your man to be smart enough to turn that down for 10-15 years of marriage? I say 15, because after 15, on average, nobody is going anywhere after that...lol... You have to remember that in a relationship you have to constantly be evolving, constantly growing, and changing. If I'm the same person that I was ten years ago, and my wife has grown, how can I expect to keep this woman? …and vice versa...*

Nate Johnson*: ...in some cases there's something that's lacking at home and he's feeling less of a man and is talked down to, and disrespected, and he's not being built up, and he's not being shown that affection... and I don't think that every situation a man goes out and looks to cheat.. I think sometimes it can start off as something innocent, but that woman sensing that he isn't getting something from home, the other woman starts to now build him up and say things that he wants to hear from his wife... and now here he is like, "Wait a minute. Here's a complete stranger, and she sees all these things..." and he is saying to himself, "How does my wife not see these things?"...sometimes it's something innocent that evolves into something and then you're around them more and more ...and then you go home, and you get the total opposite and then you're starting to shut down at home... and where you're shutting down in one place, you're opening up in another.*

Let me ask you a question, Ladies. If we had hidden cameras in your home from the time you got married up until this moment, would the audience watching your show be empathetic to seeing your husband fall for another woman? Would we see you lacking in an area where your husband needed you? When you said, "I do," you signed up to stand in the gap for all his needs and desires that a wife is responsible for. It is unacceptable for a man to neglect you and lack when it comes to your needs and desires so why is it okay for you to do this to him? Now, there are moments when life events can hinder a spouse from performing in the marriage, but it's your job to be on top of any lack that your spouse feels and do everything possible to keep your spouse focused on you. We aren't trying to scare you into thinking another woman is going to seduce your man but we are saying that you play a major part in opening and closing the door another person can so easily walk into.

To be clear, any man who cheats for any reason is selfish. Whether he experienced lack or not from his wife is irrelevant. I am of the mindset if you are unable to be faithful to your wife, grant her a divorce instead of being dishonest behind her back. It is selfish to make a woman stay married to a cheating man. If you can work it out, great but if you can't don't lie to her just leave. Selfishness is another major reason men cheat. Here's more insight from our panel.

Sam Smith: *I think we all have an animalistic nature about us and tendencies. There is evil out there in the world, and there is temptation. It's a battle and a spiritual warfare going on out there, and the devil is out to kill, steal, and destroy. If there's a way that the devil is going to try, then he will try you.*

Brian Clarke: *In the context of marriage for a non-believer, men cheat because of greed and because they're feeling the lack of something at home.. a man could have a fantastic wife but still cheat. Why? Because of greed or he could have that nagging woman or that controlling woman, and he is looking for something that he is not being provided for him at home. For a believer, it's only one answer, God was not real enough in his life... it was not a respect enough of the covenant in his life. I can give thousands of reasons or a billion reasons, but it all comes back down to not respecting the covenant and not respecting God in his life... or God was not real enough in his life.*

Rodney Lawson: *Immaturity for one. They're not ready to settle down. Their upbringing may have them in a mindset that it's okay to do that based upon what they've seen from other males in their lives... maybe their father, or... uncle, or friends that are older... Ultimately it boils down to a brokenness in a man... when a man has brokenness, sometimes he doesn't realize he's broke inside with his values... His thought process is, it's okay for him to think that he can connect with somebody just physically and not spiritually... and that connection should only be with his wife. And a lot of times, men are not thinking about what they really love and what they're really going to lose if they get caught ....and they're not thinking about that because it's a brokenness inside. It's funny that you're asking this question because I'm working with men along these lines of their brokenness, and as I had to understand my brokenness.... I'm hearing their stories, and it's amazing that a lot of this stuff transcends back to their childhood and either there was a love or lack of love or affection from their parents... and it now relates to them stepping outside in their current marriage... and then some men actually think that it's okay to do that and they don't have a sense of remorseful values towards cheating.*

Earlier, Delante said, "Men are like babies." Well, any parent knows that although a baby might be cute and cuddly, they are selfish. They want to be fed now and if you don't feed them soon you will hear them cry. Same goes for attention that babies want, talking to them, playing with them, etc... If you don't do it, they react. Well, a man is just like another child in your home. We are big, grown babies and we want what we want when we want it. Men want attention from their wives in some manner be it food, sex, conversation, advice, and the like. Of course we can be patient at times when we don't get what we are looking for but the level of patience needed to resist selfish thoughts are extremely low. And like Rodney said, if his background has some issues or his values are off, that brokenness in his mind will cause his selfish thoughts to turn into action that may result in him cheating. Additionally, if there is a lack of spirituality that Sam and Brian pointed out, you may also have a cheater on your hands.

No matter how good he may look or other needs he may be fulfilling for you, single ladies, please protect yourselves before you get married by understanding his upbringing and thought process about life from a spiritual perspective. There are generational curses that exist in every family. Yes, your man might come from a long line of cheating men. So that means there was some information planted in his DNA while he was growing up, whereas, he may think that cheating is ok. You might think this shouldn't be an issue because you do so many things for him and men just shouldn't cheat on their wives. Cheating is passed from generation to generation just like alcoholism, cancer, baldness, and athleticism. Pay attention to how he was raised and be cautious of who you are married to or who you are thinking of marrying.

Another consistent reason I heard from the panel that Delante echoed was, "but they did that to get him." This refers to the thought process that women change and do less to keep him than they did to marry him. So let's look at how some men feel about the bait-and-switch routine that men can experience once they get married.

Kevin Gray: *I think it's important for a woman to maintain their image. I know that genetics come into play when she has a child and I understand how that can change their body. But I have seen women look unbelievable and when they get into a relationship, they say, 'okay, I got him, I'm just going to let myself go…" I believe that's false advertisement. You have to be kind of like what Beyoncé said, 'keep it sexy.' That includes your body, your mind, and your spirit. Even though I understand you are at home and you are supposed to feel comfortable, but you should not have a lackluster appearance in front of your spouse too often.*

Chancey King: *For example, as long as you're pouring water into a cup it will never run empty... as long as you're filling it up, it'll always keep running over, and that's what happens in a marriage... especially with men, we need to be fed…we have egos... and you have to feed our egos. But some women say, "I don't want to do all that. I don't have to do all that…"*

and when I hear that, the number one thing I found out with couples, I will ask her, "What did you do when you first met him?"... and often times what their now doing in marriage is not what they did when they first got married... but when they first met him, and it goes the other way as well, but a big part of it is that when you first met him, "yeah, I was swinging on the chandeliers."... and now he can barely get a foot rub. What's the difference there? And sometimes women start talking about, "well, you don't know what it's like, and yeah, we have babies blah, blah, blah"... okay that can't be argued… but at the end of the day, that husband has, by design, the one that is to be fed at home when it comes down to the loving the nurturing and the care. If you forward it to him, you'll get it back because he's then going to pour it into you and into the children.

Let's go to the videotape of what you looked like while you were dating your husband. How did you keep yourself up? What were you normally wearing when he was around? What was the bedroom performance, if applicable? Now, let's pull up the video of those same questions post matrimony. What would your husband say if I asked him those questions? Are you giving him something to look at or are you comfortable and let yourself go? And please don't give that lame excuse about "babies". Every woman's body or appearance does not have to drastically change because they had a baby. And most of the women who say this, have a child who is 3-4+ years old. Not the ones who have an infant. You have an infant? It's okay. We know you have some time to work on getting back or close to how things used to look. But for the rest of you who choose to look less than that which is attractive to your husband because you have children, you're lying to yourself. You are making excuses.

If you have a 3 year old = 365 days x 3 = 1,095 days.

So you're telling your husband that in 1,095 days you couldn't find the time to get back to the level that your husband likes? 60-90 days in the gym out of 1,095 was just too much, huh? Why? Because you're married and he has to take you as you are? You're not that busy… That is selfish. And yet you're mad if he looks at another woman? When you said, "I do" you signed up to look close to, as much as possible, what he desires, as often as possible. If you are saying that's too hard, then you are opening the door for his mind to wander. And here's another point, there are plenty of women with the same number of, if not more, children than you and they keep themselves looking to the level that is appealing to your husband. And your husband knows them. So barring any health related complications, it is difficult for him to receive you bearing children as your reasoning for not keeping your physical appearance up to par.

And along those same lines, what else did you do while you were dating, that you don't do anymore with or for him? Barring any health-related issues preventing you, what would the videotape of your home life show? How do you speak to him? Do you sex him? Do you apply his love language? Or did that all change since the dating phase is over? Whatever you did to get him, you need to do for as long as you can throughout your marriage. As we get closer to elderly years sometimes things can't be done at the same level or perhaps not at all. And that's okay because your husband knows whether or not if you are capable of doing certain things like you did when you were dating. And if he loves you as a husband, then he will be empathetic or patient with this scenario. The problem is that this is usually not the case. Many women get married and get comfortable and stop doing what they used to do because they don't feel like they have to be at the top of their game and or compete anymore. Yes, I say compete because in order to get him, many of you went above and beyond to keep his focus on you so he wouldn't be distracted by another woman while you were dating. You were in competition and you "won" a husband. But in the current episodes of your marriage, you constantly fall short of meeting the expectations you agreed to. How would the viewers of your show feel about the thoughts of your husband or his actions of being with a side chick because you are too lazy or stubborn to step your game up or at least attempt to maintain as close as possible to what your husband's expectations are?

When you said, "I do" you signed up to be his bedroom vixen for life. How is your performance in that area lately? What would he say about you keeping the appeal and the sexy going? Or maybe it's the cooking, or cleaning, or whatever the case may be. What would your relationship before and after video show? I encourage you to work as hard as you can to get back to how things should be. Ask your husband to give you some ideas of things you used to do while you were dating and then work on them. This will protect your husband's mind from wondering about what you used to do and wandering towards another woman who can satisfy what you are unwilling to do.

So let's look back at Delante again as he said another key point. At this point, I'm kind of laughing while I write this because you probably thought he was crass when you first read what he said overall, but he told you exactly what we think and that goes to the last point. "Men tell you most of the time before we cheat." Now, we don't come out and say we are going to cheat. Instead, we lay down expectations of our wives and expect them to be followed. If the expectations are not followed, it opens up the door for someone else to follow the expectation or give the appearance thereof that we will be followed and that can lead a man to cheat.

Donald Bell: *Number one is having sex with your man on a regular basis. I know some men who haven't had sex with their wives in months... and the Devil is a Lie... that shan't ever happen in the Bell household. Number 2, talking down to him and disrespecting him... disrespecting him in front of his children... you want leadership in the house, but then you don't follow the leadership that's been given in the house... if we say these are the rules that pertains to the house or say this is what we're going to do about the finances, and then you go out and spend money and do stuff that we said we weren't going to do, then you open up yourself for outside forces to come in... because the side chick is going to do whatever the man tells her to do... the side chick is going to be nice ... the side chick is going to cook... the side chick is not going to spend the money... she doesn't cause no drama, be all emotional... and trust me the side chick might be at his job and can sense when y'all fussing and fighting... she's like, "What's wrong? You don't seem like yourself... and you normally come in and say good morning... and you're the bright spot in the office... and it's just like something's bothering you"... and he's like, "oh, nothing..." and then she's like, "Okay, well don't worry about it. If you want to talk or have a cup of coffee... if you just want to talk, let me know" and then a few days later she's like "okay, you know what, it's been a couple of days now and I'm not letting you sit there like this. We're going to lunch today, and I don't care what you say... it's my treat... we're going to lunch today... I don't care what you say".... and then there it is... The door's been opened.*

Donald shared with us how a man will tell you how he wants things to be or set an expectation. Now you have three choices:

1. You can do exactly what he says, which is ideal.
2. You can reach a compromise and reset the expectation with him so it at least shows collaboration and that you are attempting to satisfy his desires.
3. You can operate outside the husband's expectations with no collaboration.

So you have 3 options, and you just think because you married, and grown, and independent, that you can pick door Number 3 and your husband is going to be cool with that? Let me know how that works out for you. As a matter of fact, read the end of what Donald said above because either right now or very soon your husband will have that temptation in his ear. And it's like what Chris Jackson said earlier, if you think you can continuously fall short of your husband's expectations for 10 to 15 years and he won't step out?... Good luck with that. And when I say this to women they always say, "Well, he fell short with XYZ and I never cheated." And I'm like "okay, shame on him for falling short on XYZ and kudos to you for not cheating. But you are smarter and have a higher ability to turn down the temptation of stepping out versus your husband. I know it sounds like I am giving us a pass to disrespect the marriage. That is not what I am doing. I am merely giving you a snapshot of what goes on in your man's mind in order for you to be equipped to keep the side chick out of your man's thoughts and your marriage bed.

Men are hunters by nature, so we are used to going out and getting and doing and being the leader. Your husband is most likely used to being followed or being given the feeling that he is leading. When you choose option #3, you're not following the leader. So when another woman looks like she will follow, it becomes a challenge to resist her temptation.

Men are weaker to falling to temptation from women, than women are to men. Like a comedian once said, "ever since you were 14 years old some man has been trying to screw you." So you are more used to turning down temptation. The comedian then went on to say that men try to run from it, but we can't run that fast. So for a world renowned comedian to joke about this on stage whereas the audience was laughing and agreeing, shows that there must be some kind of truth behind his premise. And if a wife continuously lacks in an area that he has talked to you about, or you fail to meet his expectation through lack of collaboration and compromise, then you are now setting him up to possibly lose in his run to get away from that temptation. We can run, but if you don't do your part to meet the expectations he has set, don't expect us to be able to run that far. We can't run that far or fast when it comes to temptation. Yes, we are responsible for disciplining ourselves and running from temptation but please, don't push us into the arms of another woman because of lack and neglect.

The weekly television show I'd discussed in the beginning of this chapter is a microcosm of what can happen on the show of your own life. Knowing this, I will close with the question: ***How can a wife, give a side chick life?***

Donald Bell: *A wife gives the side chick life when she opens the door with her attitude… she opens it up with how she treats her man, she opens it up with not appreciating her man, she opens it up by disrespecting him... A friend of mine said something profound at a Wifeability Conference. He gave the "dog training" example. He said "some owners treat their dogs so well, that even when the door is open, or even when the gate is left unlocked, the dog never goes outside the gate because their owner treats them so well... they groom them, they give him the best food, and take good care of them... but if you've got an owner that's kicking the dog, don't feed the dog, don't take care of the dog... as soon as that gate is open, he's going to shoot out of there like a bat out of hell"... and that's how wives can give life to the side chick by mistreating their husbands and opening up that door... now, there is a responsibility for the man to keep things in check and not even go there with the side chick, but you can give life to the side chick if you are mistreating your husband and neglecting him. When I say mistreating him, I mean disrespecting him, not abiding by the guidelines of the household, disrespecting him in front of the children... and like I said, it's not just mistreating him, it's neglect, too... some of these women are so career-oriented and that's great, but never be so busy to whereas you're not taking care of home... if you're going to be gone, make sure that there are some meals prepared for the next couple of days so he can just warm it up... because the side chick will make sure that he eats... believe that... you don't have any food at work, and she's like, "you know what, I noticed that you didn't have your Tupperware here the last couple of days, I want to make sure that you ate, so I made you a little something from home..." lol... it is real out in these streets...*

If the gate was opened in your home, how would your husband react? Be mindful of your participation in the episodes in your home. Take heed to the information these men have shared so that you can protect your household from any type of unnecessary scandal that may occur.

Empowerment Tools:

- Men may cheat because of lack of something at home
- Men may cheat due to selfishness
  - Be cautious of his family background with infidelity
  - Be mindful of his spirituality level as this will reduce his selfish thoughts
- Whatever you did while dating, maintain that through marriage
- When he sets the expectations, he is saying that you need to follow these.
  - Failure to follow him is opening the door for another woman to tempt him
- Do not give the side chick life by falling short of maintaining your man

Learn to speak your man's language and he will learn to speak yours. This is a recipe for building a lasting relationship.

CHAPTER 11

Speaking My Language

I'D BEEN MARRIED about a year or so when my wife Michelle and I were sitting in our kitchen having a general conversation. Somehow we started talking about my mother and some of the things Michelle used to discuss with her. My wife said, "Your mother told me one day that you need a lot of encouragement." I replied, "What do you mean?" She said, "Your mom told me that if I'm going to be with you that I have to be ready to stay in your ear and give you a lot of encouragement." She said, "if you do it right, Elam will run through a brick wall for you." I remember pausing and trying to make sense of this. Here I was twenty-six or twenty-seven years old and I'd never heard anyone say that about me. I thought to myself, "is that true? I didn't know that." I mean, of course, being encouraged feels good but how did my mom know to break this down to my wife? Why did she think that was so important to tell her? My wife and I talked for a few more minutes but never discussed it further.

I grew up in a middle-class family. I have five brothers. My mom was a teacher and my dad owned his own maintenance, snow plowing, and landscaping business. My parents rarely, if ever, hung out. They didn't wear name brand clothing. If they weren't working or caring for something in the home, they were watching TV or exercising in their leisure time. For Christmas, we would either get one gift each, or we might get one gift to share with another sibling or one gift for all of us to share. My family lived a very conservative life, therefore, I had a high level of respect for money and was very cautious about what I spent it on. As I got older and got a job, I never spent too much money on women. I used to sit and listen to stories from women on how their man would spend all this money on them or they would take the money the guy would give them and take me out to dinner or buy me things. I remember thinking how stupid those guys were and how I would never spend money on anyone I wasn't married to. Some of you may probably call me cheap...lol

When Michelle and I started dating, I took this same concept into our relationship. We would hang out and do dinner or movie, paddle boating, golfing, and the like but buying her things was not my style. And at the time, I was making what many people would consider "good money" so needless to say I could afford to spend money on her if I wanted to.

Two years into dating, we took a trip to Atlanta. I remember going shopping and spending $1,000 to $2000.00 on clothes for myself. She also purchased a few high-end items for herself as well. When we were almost finished shopping, we were standing at the counter and I was about to pay for my items. She picked up a hair clip that cost about three to four dollars and she asked, "Can you get this for me?" I looked at her and hesitated, and she looked back at me smiling. I said a few words and then said, "Okay." I will never forget how her face lit up. I finished paying for the items and as we walked out of the store she said, "I'm so happy about my hair clip." I said, "Why? It's just a hair clip." She said, "Because this is the first thing you've ever bought for me." I shook my head and I remember thinking, "Don't get used to it."

One of the topics I felt important to discuss is the 5 Love Languages. If you are not familiar with the love languages don't feel bad. I was married for about 7 years before my wife played a CD discussing them. Here are the love languages in no particular order:

- Words of Affirmation
- Physical Touch
- Gifts
- Quality Time
- Acts of Kindness or Service

There are manuals and research you can read online to get a more in-depth understanding of these languages. Most people have the tendency to like all the love languages at some point in their relationship and throughout life, but there is a priority level that each person has. You always have a primary and a secondary love language at any given point. It represents the way you give love and receive love from people. For example, my mother knew that I was a "Words of Affirmation" person. Even though she never talked to us about these languages, she figured it out as I was growing up. On the contrary, considering that my parents never lavished us with gifts nor placed much emphasis on gift-giving, the language of gifts was at the bottom of my list.

This is not to say that your parents are the sole reason for the development of your love language but I do believe my upbringing had a lot to do with how I viewed giving and receiving gifts. It's not that I was cheap when I was dating, I just didn't give or receive love in that manner but after learning about the love languages, I understood why Michelle was so happy about the hair clip that day.

Allow me to share with you the importance of understanding your man's love language. The question I asked the panel was, ***"How do you feel about love languages playing a role in your relationship?"***

Chris Jackson:... *the more that you choose to understand the other person, the better you are at making sure that person has their needs met. I feel that people who overlook this miss an opportunity to connect with their significant other. We can't see the world only through our own lenses. We have to look outside of that. We have to be able to see the world through the other person's lenses as well and that allows us to better meet their needs... But if you're constantly looking at them through only your eyes, you're going to miss the other person.*

Donald Bell: *I think that the whole "Love Language" series as a tool in your marriage is absolutely essential. I think you should study and grasp all five of the love languages... do you necessarily have to get with somebody who has the same Love Languages? Well, 9 times out of 10 you're not because opposites attract. So, you're probably not going to be with someone who has the exact same Love Languages as you do…. and I don't think that's necessary... but I do think it's essential that you understand all of the love languages and understand what your spouse's Love Language is and what your love language is so you can make sure you're communicating to her in her love language and then she's communicating to you in your love language... unless you're doing it in their love language they don't hear you... so if their love language is Acts of Service and you're trying to love them with Words of Affirmation then you're sounding like the teacher on Charlie Brown (wah, wah, wah)...or if you want physical touch and she's coming with Words of Affirmation you're like, "you can miss me with all that... what I need you to do right now is drop it like it's hot right now"...lol...*

Rodney Lawson: *I think it should play a very prominent role in all relationships. If I'm thinking about my own relationships, I will say that I have screwed up in the past because I did not understand my significant other's Love Language. You can't continue to get your needs met if you don't even understand what the needs of your significant others are...and we have a habit of showing our love in our own language versus showing it in our significant others language... For example, one time I bought my wife three pairs of designer shoes at one time. That still did not keep her wanting to be married to me.... see my love language was gifts and hers was not... and to be honest it wasn't until I went through the book about love languages that I realized how important it is.*

What I think is important here is how the men are talking about not only the importance of love languages in a relationship but also loving each other in that person's respective language as well. It cannot be a one-way street, whereas, you are only loving them in your respective love language. As you can see from Rodney and Donald's examples that is not going to work. Additionally, you are not going to change someone else's love language. You have to love that person the way they need to be loved.

Rafiq Shakur: *I firmly believe that love language plays a part in a relationship. If you can understand what makes a person feel good, that's really what love languages are about... How you express it and how you receive it. A part of a relationship is understanding what makes your partner or your spouse feel good. How I put out my love language is how most men do it, whereas, acts of kindness is what most men do and that's primarily how we show love to our mates... but I have to be open to the fact that that may not do it for the woman that I'm with. She may look at it and say, "yeah, I kind of appreciate you doing acts for me but you still didn't move me as if you sit down and watch a movie with me"...that may have more significance. When she understands that I'm not operating in my own love language anymore, I'm operating inside of her love language. For example, sitting down watching that movie may not mean a hill of beans for somebody who wants you to fix their car, but maybe it gets more value if it gets received in the context that I'm trying to operate inside of her love language.*

I want to highlight Rafiq's point about Acts of Kindness or Service. I will take it a step further and add Gifts in there as well. I think these two languages are what men are mostly taught as we were growing up that women wanted in a relationship. Yes, we understand the importance of Quality Time, Physical Touch, and Words of Affirmation, but we are taught to "do" for a woman. Doing involves Acts of Kindness or Service or buying her something. We walk into the relationship thinking that these are the norms for what will make women happy. We think, "If I buy her something or fix her car or do something nice for her then I am showing her love". Well, it's clear that there are three other languages we should be keeping in mind, however, we are creatures of habit and we just don't know what we don't know.

Let's think about Valentine's Day. This is the day where advertising efforts encourage (scare) a man into buying something for his woman or reminding him to do something with her. Notice how there are millions of roses, balloons and all types of heart-shaped candy combinations on sale but on average these are NOT the things that most men want. Even in elementary school, little boys see Valentine's Day as a day to do something sweet for his "crush". We are conditioned from a young age to do or buy for women. So where am I going with this?

The conditioning that boys receive from society can be dangerous particularly because we either don't know the other love languages or we are not in tune with other ways that women may give or receive love. For example, all of the men on my panel are what I consider highly educated or very astute men, however, over half of the men didn't know what the love languages were. Some had heard of them but had forgotten what they were. On the contrary, many women have heard of the love languages and have used them as a litmus test in their relationships to determine whether or not a man truly loves her.

Single ladies, ask the next guy you meet what his love language is and you share yours with him at the appropriate time. Not necessarily on the first date but if you can see yourself with this guy long-term, find out his love capacity. This should be done in the very beginning of the relationship like we discussed in Chapter 4, "Do You See Me". This will give you an opportunity to discover whether or not you can provide that type of love in the relationship on a consistent basis I encourage wives to find out your husband's love language if you don't know it and you share yours with him. Most of the time men will not bring this topic up proactively. To be clear, anything talking about the subject of love is not what the average guy is going to discuss in a new or tenured relationship.

So please, take the lead in this regard and guide the man in the understanding of what your love needs are. You may need to reinforce the importance of love languages in the relationship periodically because he is most likely going to forget. When I say periodically, I mean for you to let him know when he is actively engaging in your love language. Even a simple statement like, "This is what makes me feel loved by you" will resonate in his mind and he will try to repeat it as often as possible.

Now, I caution you that you should be realistic as well as careful of how you present and reinforce the love languages in your relationship. For example, if your love language is Gifts and you know that he may be having some temporary financial challenges, you should be careful of the expectations you set here. If your man knows you like gifts and he can't afford them, he already knows it. So if you bring it up, I can bet you that 99% of the time that conversation will turn into an argument. This advice is not so much for the discovery of the love languages, as it is for reinforcement of what your love languages are for your relationship ongoing. If you share your love languages with one another in the beginning, it's up to both the man and the woman to make the decision to continue forward or end the relationship.

Porter Bingham: *I feel like that at any given day, whatever your primary or secondary love language is, I think that you have to try to stay in tune with the person and be willing to try to approach them wherever they are at any given point in time. For example, right now my wife's parents are having some health challenges and I know what may have worked for her 6 months ago may not work for her right now... I don't know if it's "touch" that might do it... acts of kindness might not do it because it's hard to work with that distress... quality time is something that I should probably ramp up just so she can have a sounding board to go through these things…so I think that at different points based upon your life and your relationship all of those Love Languages have an appropriate time.*

Chancey King: *...I look at it as like building a house. If you're going to build it together, you both know that there are certain components that you want in it. The problem is that you don't know what size and where you want the home... you know you need bathrooms and showers and the kitchen but once you start putting all the components in place, you find out that there's going to be a lot of give-and-take, a lot of mixing and matching and you find out what's going to work and you find out what environment the four walls can be created that both of you* *can live in and it starts with love, period... And then, you have to figure it out from there as you learn each other... and it does not stay that way... sometimes it changes over a matter of years and just like in the home example, sometimes there's remodeling in the home because things have changed. I believe that this is analogous to a relationship. I do not believe a relationship stays the same... it develops in the course... it inflates in some areas and deflates in other areas and you have to adjust and tweak it as you go. So from my experience, if you're trying to go right into the relationship with the love languages and you're trying to stick to the script, I think that you will miss it many times because it can evolve and change.*

I want to end this chapter with making sure you stay in tune with the evolution of your mate's love language. Allow me to reiterate that men are not as free-flowing with the evolution of their feelings. So this means you will not only have to nurture the development of the love languages in your relationships, but also the ongoing temperature checks of how your man is receiving and giving love. I would say the biggest benefit for you here is that as you check on his love language, it will allow you to reinforce the existing language you already told him about or you can communicate to him your new or updated language. Your nurturing of the love languages will take the guesswork out of communicating your needs to him and it will show him that you are willing to evolve with his needs as well. That's a win-win situation for your relationship. Don't assume that your man is smart enough to know you have evolved. Nurture him in this area and he will eventually follow. Learn to speak your man's language and he will learn to speak yours. This is a recipe for building a lasting relationship.

Empowerment Tools:

- Know and remain educated about the 5 Love Languages.
- Learn each other's love languages early in the relationship
- Reinforce with care and be mindful of his ability to satisfy your love language
- Single Ladies, terminate the relationship early on if you don't think he can apply your love language
- Married Ladies, be patient and understand that your love languages will evolve with time and will need your periodic leadership

As your brothers, we authorize, entitle, permit, allow, license, sanction, warrant, commission, delegate, qualify, enable, and equip you to take the lead on being the Relationship Enhancement Officer in the marriage.

CHAPTER 12

Relationship Enhancement Is Your Responsibility

IF SOMEONE CONFIDED in you about their relationship and said, "We are in counseling", what would your initial thought be? The word "counseling" has a stigma that something must be wrong in the relationship. Many of us were taught that seeking counsel must mean that we don't have it all together. There's a misnomer that if we're going to counseling, it must mean that things are about to end. We can't tell anyone that we are in counseling so we continue to lie about our status and smile for the cameras.

Let's talk about pre-marital counseling. After getting engaged, how many people proactively attend counseling services? How many people go to premarital counseling at all? How many people pay top dollar to have a Counselor assess their spiritual, emotional, mental, and financial compatibility while simultaneously planning the wedding? Some individuals may speak with their pastor or a counselor a few times, but seeking counsel is usually not the primary focus. Many of us are more concerned with the dress, the wedding venue, the guest list, and the rest of the wedding day festivities when meanwhile, there may be some hidden and/or unknown issues that are buried inside the relationship that needs to be discussed immediately.

People fail to realize that long after the wedding bells ring, the work begins. If you didn't know, let me share with you that marriage takes work. It is a full-time job with no days off. It takes a special skillset to execute a successful, thriving, lasting marriage on a daily basis. Who you marry is the most important decision you will ever make in your life. But somehow we get caught up in the short-term planning of the wedding festivities....the glitz, the glamour and the optics when we should be focused on the initial assessment of the relationship as well as the long-term maintenance of the marriage. It is imperative that engaged couples deem pre-marital counseling more important than the wedding itself.

If you say the words, "Elam, I just got engaged!" and after congratulating you I am going to exclaim with the same level of excitement, "GO TO COUNSELING!" Hire the best counselor you can find and go to work on your preliminary understanding and the necessities it will take to make the relationship last. If you don't do counseling.... And I don't mean one or two sessions.... I mean at least five to ten sessions.... If you don't do counseling, you are setting your marriage up for failure. You need to have a neutral party come in and make sure that you two are on the same page. It doesn't matter the number of years you've been dating or if you have children together. You may even share a house, a car, and may be great business partners but you need someone to help the two of you establish standard operating procedures of roles, responsibilities, and expectations when it comes to the marriage on a day to day basis.

Marriage is not for everyone, therefore, it's imperative that you find out as much as you can about your mate before marriage because the toughest part of any relationship is discovering that it's not going to work. Counseling may reveal blind spots you may have or things you may have missed prior to becoming engaged. It's okay to get out now. It is much better for you to know who you are dealing with before getting married than to endure the heartache, headache, and possible legal issues to deal with after marriage.

The question I asked the panel was, ***"Do you feel that ongoing marriage seminars and counseling are important for your marriage or should you only seek help when there is a problem?"***

Omar Finley: *I think that ongoing [support] is very important. It's almost like water. People need water every day...you need a marriage seminar at least once a month or a quarter. You need to listen to somebody who has a good marriage because when you have problems in your marriage, it feels like it's the end of the world, and the truth is it's an opportunity to grow...*

Trey Barnette: *I think that it should be on going and I think that it shouldn't just only touch the intimacy or how to run a family. I think that the big part about it should be the finances and how you run the family business because that is a big part of it. A large percentage of divorces are created because of some type of financial challenges... so I think those seminars and workshops about intimacy are good, but I think that more should be added to them than just the traditional intimacy issues or problem-solving...*

Barry Case: *I recommend that it's on going and just like anything else everything needs maintenance... you don't get an oil change just once or every so often...any type of company that's successful, we have weekly meetings, we have quarterly meetings where we're projecting, we're forecasting, The employees and the staff are constantly going through training and getting better... you can't just have a relationship and not employ those types of tactics and expect it to be successful. You will not develop as a woman, and as a spouse, and as a husband, you have to constantly be getting better and you have to develop. It doesn't always have to be formal. It can be informal. It might be conversations with one of your frat brothers like you and I talk. You have to surround yourself with other people who are purposeful and trying to be successful. It doesn't always mean we have to go to a conference or we have to be sitting down with the minister, or reading a book…even if it's watching certain things on TV that edifies marriage... I feel like you need to constantly be doing that.*

For those of who played a sport in school, did your coach let you play in a game if you didn't come to practice? How many people played in the band on game day when they didn't come to band practice prior to the game? Before you took a test, did you study to ensure you had the answers down, or at least do some research to ensure you were properly prepared for the test? Who has ever owned a car and drove it without doing any maintenance to the vehicle? Prior to cooking a dish that you have never made, shouldn't you research the best recipe in order to successfully cook the dish? When you're on your job and you want to be promoted, wouldn't you go back to school or perhaps study under someone else to improve your skill set? So why is it we are so diligent when it comes to these areas but when it comes to our marriages, maintenance is an afterthought? With our marriages, we are apprehensive or fail to do our due diligence to improve individually nor collectively. We make everything else a priority in our lives and there is something wrong with that thought process. We've got to do better.

For those of you who may be saying, "Well, I want to improve but he doesn't want to or he's not working in the area I want to work in", here's the thing, there are some people who don't want to get better. Period. There are two reasons why people don't change, either they don't know how, or they don't want to. Ladies, your job is to help your man with the "don't know how". I know we can be stubborn, egomaniacs, selfish, immature, and the list goes on but my advice is to work on the "don't know how" portion of your marriage as best you can. Seminars, books, conferences, counseling, whatever it takes...give it all you've got.

Society has taught women to be knowledgeable and vigilant when it comes to dreams, goals, and even in the raising of your children. But the maintenance of your marriage comes first. I am fully aware that there are some marriages that are just over and probably never should have started in the first place but we need to stop acting like the institution of marriage is not worth proactively fighting for because it is. You don't want to wait until your engine blows to put oil in it, right? You don't wait until your child flunks out of school to get them tutoring, right? You don't wait until the Thanksgiving Turkey is dry to baste it, right? Take the lead and seek wisdom to prevent your marriage's engine from blowing. Take the initiative to prevent your relationship from receiving a failing grade. Don't wait for your intimacy dry up before proactively involving yourself and your spouse in an ongoing relationship maintenance plan.

I also asked the panel an additional question regarding relationship maintenance and their daughters which was, **"what would you recommend your daughter do to continuously enhance her marriage?"**

Omar Finley: *I would tell my daughter to read. Read all the time. Read everything that you can get your hands on about marriage from people that you can research that have a good marriage. A lot of people write marriage books, and I've read a lot of crap and I've read a lot of mess out there... and I would read the book and I say to myself, "why the heck am I reading this?"... but then I have also read books that take it to another level. I read a lot of books when I was in network marketing and to be honest with you if I had never gotten into network marketing I probably never even would have gotten married... I was trying to be successful and I messed around and became a man...*

Chris Jackson: *I would recommend to her to ask questions. Never think that you got it all figured out. For example, when you hear people say, 'oh, I know him, or oh, I know her', you begin to get too comfortable in your space... and I don't mean just ask questions about the other person. You also need to ask questions about yourself as well... and that doesn't mean you just ask questions about where is the lack... you should also ask questions [like], "what is working for us right now? ... and then also ask, "Why is it working?" ... but we have to be willing to constantly challenge ourselves and challenge our relationship.*

John Telley Gilliard: *You should do preventative maintenance. My wife wanted to do something different a couple years ago. She wanted to do something every six months... we should re-evaluate our marriage, write down what do we need to improve on and what's an opportunity or a challenge for us... Every marriage needs a preventative maintenance. Sometimes it's counseling, sometimes it's just having a conversation in that manner. Every couple should have some type of open forum to discuss the strengths, challenges, and the areas of opportunities... you need to do a S.W.O.T analysis on your own household. We have to ask ourselves, why is it that people will do a S.W.O.T analysis for their business, but they won't do it for their marriage?... and sometimes it's just too much effort... sometimes when you have to clean out your own closet you just have to see how much is really in there and you don't want to have to deal with it. Think about when we were kids. Our parents told us all the time, "Clean your room"... but at the same time sometimes your room is so messy you were just like, "S***, I don't want to do this... and sometimes it's messy to the point where you say, "I have to clean my room"... and you know you need to clean it, but it's really the effort that's involved. It's harder to look at what your own self and what's involved and what's in your own backyard versus seeing what problems other people have. My wife talks about this all the time, it's easier to give advice than it is to accept it because outside looking in you can always see what another person's problem are, but when you internalize it, it's a battle between, do I accept what I know to be true, versus what I need to improve…sometimes people block out areas in their lives so they don't have to deal with it*

Brian Clarke: *Continue to date. Continue to pour into your spouse, and allow your spouse to grow because the person that you've married in year one or two is not going to be the same person that they'll be in year nine or 10...I'll tell my daughter as you're growing individually, you're growing together. Allow yourself and your spouse a chance to grow and hopefully he'll allow you to grow... and so it becomes like a dance where you're weaving in and out together allowing for different growths. For example, my wife is not the same as when we got married... she's not the same person that she was 7 months ago... because where she's gone in God…. it's crazy.…and so it's growth... and so I'm right there with her whereas I'm not the same dude... so I would tell my daughter to continue to talk and make sure you have communication and allow your spouse to grow and encourage him to allow you to grow as well. Let the Holy Spirit do the work in the changes that you want to see in your spouse. Communicate with your spouse. Be your spouse's biggest prayer warrior with them, and also in your private time.*

Once you are married, the work starts the moment you say, "I do." And just like any other situation that you have ever dealt with in your life, you need ongoing support, knowledge, and wisdom to help you maintain the most important decision you will ever make with another person. Be prayerful, and vigilant about who you allow to speak over and into your relationship. Any advice that causes division within your marriage should be immediately rejected. Treat the advancement and development of your marriage with the same mindset you approach everything else. When you become an active participant in making your marriage better, the benefits you will reap are far beyond anything that you have ever experienced with anything else you have ever done. Every relationship has its own set of challenges but what we all share is the desire to experience exponential growth, joy, pleasure, and happiness so I encourage you to make seminars, counseling, and marriage mentorship a staple in your marriage.

Ladies, I am challenging you to take the lead in this area because as I have said numerous times throughout this manual that you are the smartest person in the relationship. One of the words in the subtitle for this manual is "empower". Empower by definition means to give someone the authority or power to do something; make someone stronger and more confident, especially in controlling their life and claiming their rights. As your brothers, we authorize, entitle, permit, allow, license, sanction, warrant, commission, delegate, qualify, enable, and equip you to take the lead on being the Relationship Enhancement Officer in the marriage. Be strong in your marriage and control your life while inside your marriage. You have a right to have a progressive, happy, loving marriage but that takes work. And although your husband is the head of the household, you are the neck of the relationship. You possess the ability to point your husband's attention to the areas of the relationship that need maintenance. You see things we don't see. You sense a storm coming far before it arrives. You possess the power to maximize your marriage by being the licensed and authorized delegate to enhance your marriage through proactive maintenance. This is not a pass for your husband to sit back and let you do all of the work but you are the one with the intuitive nature to let us know in a loving and respectful way that there is work to be done.

Empowerment Tools:

- Hire a Therapist the moment you accept a marriage proposal to explore any hidden issues that may have gone undetected in the dating process
- After marriage, engage in ongoing seminars, counseling, and relationship management
- Ladies are encouraged to take the lead on proactively implementing the tools necessary to keep the marriage properly maintained and constantly flourishing as the Relationship Enhancement Officer.

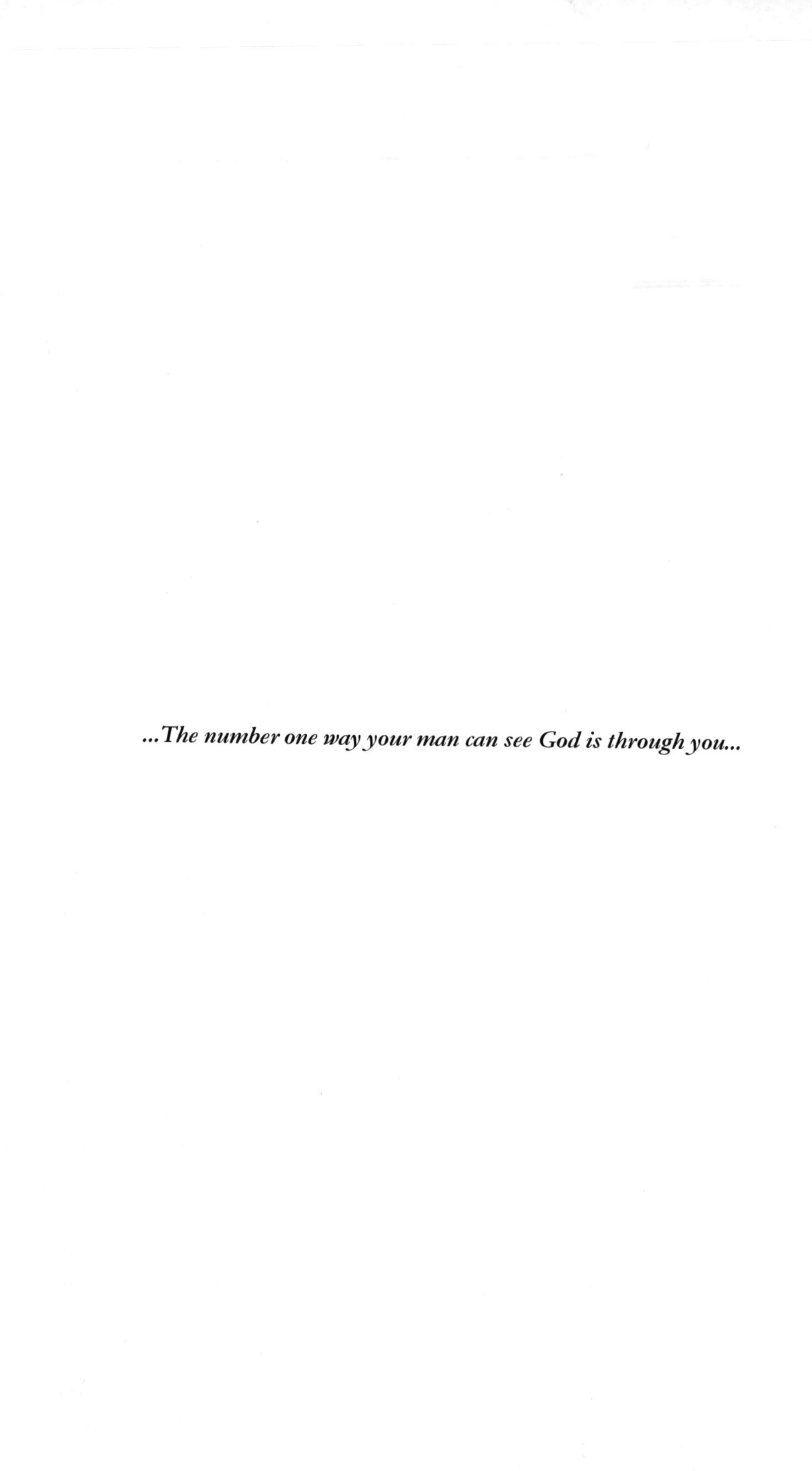

...The number one way your man can see God is through you...

Chapter 13

The Importance of Spirituality in Your Relationship

Traditionally, in many communities, believing in God or a higher power of some sort, was a major factor in choosing a life partner. I believe that we may be moving away from this important characteristic that our mates should possess. The question I posed to the men was: **How important is it for both men and women to be spiritually grounded in a relationship?**

Before we get into understanding the answers here, I'd like to highlight two definitions. The words, "religion" and "spirituality" are often used interchangeably but they have two very different meanings and functions. Religion is defined as, "relating to or believing in a religion or particular deity", whereas, Spirituality is defined as, "the quality of being concerned with the human spirit or soul as opposed to material or physical things". There is a huge difference between Religion and Spirituality. Religion gives you permission to go through legalistic motions of proving your relationship with your higher power, whereas, Spirituality gives you the opportunity to be free and intimate with the deity your heart worships. Is religion important in a relationship? Donald Bell doesn't seem to think so. He said, "*...I definitely won't say that religion is important because we live in a very religious society, meaning I go to church, I go through these ritualistic practices, I do this....I don't do this...I don't do that, and therefore I have a relationship with God... so I won't say that religion is important, but I will say that a relationship and intimacy with God is important because religion and intimacy with God are two different things.*

This chapter is not about attempting to convert you to any specific religion. Of the men on the panel, we have a mixed group of Christians, Muslims, and other belief systems, who have shared their experiences which I think is key to highlight because everyone is not going to have the same belief system that you have. That does not mean that you cannot give or receive advice or insight from those who have a different belief system. It is possible to worship a different deity but share the same life principles. This is not to say that you should go out and find a Christian man if you are a Muslim woman but the purpose of this chapter is to highlight the importance of spirituality in your relationship.

As we look at relationships in today's modern world, we have gotten so caught up in what society says, and we have become ashamed or apprehensive about having spirituality as a prerequisite as we choose a mate. It is the human responsibility to be concerned with the human spirit or soul. Spirituality should be the number one priority that a man and woman should look for as well as possess when choosing a mate. Another question I posed to the panel was, "**What do they think the importance is in having spirituality when choosing your mate? Do you think both parties should be spiritually grounded?**

Sam Smith*: I think you have to be. God should be the foundation for any marriage. God has always been there for me through the good times and through the bad times, particularly through the rough times... when my back was against the wall and I prayed to God I was able to find a way...when I didn't know what direction to turn I prayed to God and then I was given a way... and not just only for challenges, it's also for good times of watching good become great and giving thanks along the way... The benefits are there and I believe that I can do all things through Christ.*

Delante Murphy: *I think both parties need to be spiritually grounded. I think that's a part of the dating phase and outside of the dating, you need to be able to pray together and seek God. You have to understand that when your mate says, "I need to go seek God on this…" and I literally need that space before I make a decision, you have to be able to respect that. If you're a Christian and your mate is atheist, they're going to be like, "Bump your God" …..then they [are] looking down on your belief [system]… that's not going to work either.*

Raasan Austin: *If you would have asked me this question a month ago I probably would have said, "Who cares?"... but I think that there is something to some type of spirituality and for you to be evenly yoked...I think it's a necessity. I think being connected to any higher power is a good thing, but if you're going to be with somebody it would make a lot more sense to be connected to the same higher power and those same ideas, ideologies, and beliefs.*

Rafiq Shakur: *Well, the problem in the question is that it's not exclusive. Being a Christian is not as equal as being spiritually grounded. I know, depending on your perspective, we have 2 separate pieces here be it religion from spirituality. I think you would agree as a Christian you could be a Christian and not be any more spiritual than a man on the moon. I think that it is important for a woman to find a spiritually grounded man. I grew up in a household where there was Islam and Christianity and my parents made sure we read... so when I hear kids complain about just reading the Bible, whereas, in my household we had to read the Bible and the Torah and the Quran and we had to learn to speak between the three of them... that being said, the spiritual thing has to be in place. That's why I say I'm not stuck on what the ideology is... what you have to have is a spiritual foundation of some type… otherwise, we're not going to be equally yoked.*

Brian Clarke: *People get married all the time and religion is or isn't important to them, but for me it was Paramount. It was the Baseline. For my wife, it was the Baseline for her as well... so when we started off dating, I remember the first few weeks we were dating and getting into each other and we wrote out a list of everything that we wanted spiritually from a spouse. We still have that list to this day. It's important to me and it's foundational with Christ at the center of everything that we do. There's not a day that we don't leave the house without praying for one another and I send her a scripture every day... and we're not "Jesus Freaks" ...lol... we live our life and we just know who the center is. There's nothing sexier than waking up or coming into the room and your wife is in the Word… I'm like "wow, she's doing it for herself..." I don't have to prod her. I don't have to encourage her. She's doing it herself. She has also watched the things that her husband does, so she's mirroring the things that she sees me do and now she's taking ahold of it herself... We're still the same ignorant, funny fools, but we know who our center is...lol...The benefits have increased for us. We talked about the whole intimacy thing earlier and I want to say that you can't get any more intimate than just sitting there, two people in the room, holding hands, praying to God, and praying for one another to God in front of each other... so even when things have been tough and we have challenges it's that Word and it's that intimacy together that has kept us tight... Nothing but the Word.*

Ladies, allow me to empower you in this moment by saying that YOU are the ones who set the tone when it comes to what you will and will not accept in a relationship. Why is this the woman's job? Because as a man chooses to date you, he is dating you based on what you will accept from him. It is 100% impossible for you to demand a characteristic of a man and still be required to stay with him or make him your life partner. Who you choose to be with and what you choose to accept is totally up to you. For example, if you accept a drug dealer, he already knows how he is going to treat you. If you accept the "Momma's Boy" who runs to his parents when times get tough, that is what he will be throughout your relationship. If you accept the man who has no vision of where he will be in 5 or 10 years then be prepared to live a life with no vision. If you accept a man who you require to be spiritually grounded, then that is who you will attract. Do not compromise on your man being spiritually grounded. This is not to say that he should be perfect or without mistakes but he can be on the journey to be more spiritually mature on a day to day basis. **Why is it important that women are spiritually grounded and how can couples remain spiritually connected?** Kevin Gray said, "*I think that it is very important for a woman to be spiritually grounded. The reason why that I think that it is important is because you're not always going to agree on certain things, and the Bible is that spiritual authority that you need. His Word (God's Word) is the authority. If both of you are living [according] to His word, then you should be on the same page. When you see a couple worshiping together that is a very good sign things are going in the right direction. If there are any problems in your relationship, I highly suggest that you should go to church together. It's not about what you want, and it's not about what she wants, it's about what God wants. Your hands are praising him, and your defenses are down, and she's doing the exact same thing you are. And once you take the onus off of each other and put it on the Creator, then He will, in turn, start the healing process of whatever it is that you guys may be going through.*"

Marriage can be difficult to maintain should you choose religion over spirituality. Donald Bell said, "…*The intimacy with God is vital and essential because there is insight and strength that is needed to maintain your marriage that can only come from God... it is a three-fold cord one cord as your wife, 1 cord you, and the other cord has to be God... and that's what you guys align yourself around and that's the cord and the string that can't be easily broken because God has to be the centrifugal force in your relationship. In our early days, we were very religious. We went to church...matter fact we went to church more so in the early days of our relationship more than we do now. but we had less of a relationship with God then... so because of that, our relationship suffered early on... we were at church for 4-5 nights out of the week, but we weren't experiencing a level of intimacy with God... We were consistent in our service and we carried out our task and our responsibility, and we paid our tithes, but as far as seeking a deeper relationship with Him, we were missing that part. It wasn't until we sought an intimate relationship that we saw things click, and then that's when things improved in our relationship... back then we were going through a constant cycle... things will be good for a couple of months, two, three months, and then a month of hell... and it will be good for like 3 or 4 months, and then we have another month of hell... and we did that cycle for a while. But it's only been since we've had this quest to keep God first and have an intimate relationship with him that we have had less of those bumps in the road. I'm not going to front like we don't still have those bumps, but they've been less frequent...and when we have those bumps, we're able to maneuver through them, and process them, and move forward... whereas, before, we had a bump in the road and everything stopped for like a month-and-a-half, two months... and we didn't have any progress like we do now."*

Ladies, your relationship and particularly your marriage will go through cycles. During those cycles, the head of your household must have the ability to seek guidance from God first as well as seek counsel from those he trusts as spiritual leaders. Your husband must also be able to trust your spiritual maturity as he may need to obtain guidance from you from time to time. As for me, I am a Christian man who totally depends on God for wisdom, insight, knowledge, and understanding. I know that I cannot be the husband, father, son, brother, or friend I need to be aside from God, The Creator. The bottom line is your man needs to have the character and understanding that he needs his deity for guidance. So when those tough times come... And they will come...sometimes prayer and faith are all that you have to stand on. Being grounded spiritually will provide you with the comfort in knowing that you can trust your man to seek wisdom and godly counsel to help conquer the tough times.

Some of you may be saying, "Okay, Elam. That sounds great but where are these, "spiritually grounded" men?" Some of you may even be saying, "I go to church every week but my husband refuses to go with me. I am tired of trying to help him grow spiritually so I will just do my own thing." Ladies, let me share something with you; I remember hearing from more than one pastor on how the average church is normally financially sustained by women. The membership of most churches are women. On any given Sunday, you will find more women present than men. Why is that? One of the main reasons is that women, by nature, possess a higher propensity to submit to authority. When you choose a level of spirituality to follow, you have to submit your will to the deity you serve. So if by nature women inherently find it easier to submit, this is the major reason why you find more women worshipping in most religions versus men. It is also one of the major challenges that women run into when they are trying to go to church, and they find some struggles in trying to encourage her mate to attend with her. Sometimes the man is battling something internally and he is struggling with submission. Sometimes he may struggle with the teachings of the lessons he is hearing or he feels incapable of meeting the expectation. So instead of submitting, he becomes rigid and full of pride. The man's lack of humility and submission in the area of spirituality may result in his lack of attendance in church, his lack of studying the spiritual lessons shared with him or his lack of actively pursuing a relationship with God. Omar Finley shared a very transparent moment with us regarding his thoughts on spirituality by saying, "*The reason why I removed myself from church is because I felt like I couldn't grow sitting there, and I felt like if I left my family sitting there that I couldn't take them where I want them to go. What was being preached was a message of how we went from being God's people and God's children to a message of just grace and mercy. Our pastor has been speaking about grace for the past 6 years... and I know what the grace of God is, but I'd like to know what my role is in his kingdom and I want to associate myself with the Almighty directly. I want to know who I am in Christ so that I can execute in that way so I can move in my calling and be so strong in my calling, that I don't need to pursue anything but what I'm called for... and I felt like church was hindering that. I feel like church was making it difficult because you still preaching the same old message that I heard as a little boy about, "the grace of God, and God will do it, and Jesus did everything, and that it's already done"...and then I'm asking, "okay, where do I come in?"*"

Ladies, your man desires to take your family to the next level. He wants to be the driving force to make the shift that your household needs. The problem is that on Sunday or whatever day you may worship, there is someone telling him things that he needs to do. And although you may be able to receive those teachings as truth, your husband may get caught in the dogma of what is, and what should be. Although the words spoken may be the truth, most men are looking for the last sentence Omar said, "Where do I come in?" And because he doesn't have that answer, he would rather disengage versus pursue the journey of how to fit God in his everyday life. He already has to deal with life challenges such as work, home, fatherhood, friendships, and other societal factors but those other factors are tangible to him. He can see his work, kids, friends, and the like, but he can't see God or the importance spirituality. So which do you think becomes the last of his priorities?

Ladies, here's where your spirituality comes in. The number one way your man can see God is through you. How you act and conduct yourself in your household is an indication of where God is in your life and how strong he can be in his life as well. How you deal with your job, friends, children, and life be it challenges or successes, is an indication of how spirituality can work for him as well. Many of you know what it takes and may know better of what is needed. If you want the right man to choose you or if you desire a deeper level of spirituality in your relationship, you need to maximize your submission to the one you worship. As you do this, you will notice one of two things. Either the man you love will get on board and strengthen his relationship with God or you will be led in a direction that is most positive to the potential of where you need to be and who you need to be with. Single Ladies, can your potential mate trust the God in you? Married Ladies, can your husband see the God in you? This is not a call for you to be perfect either but it is a clarion call for you to be the spiritual example a man can count on.

The number one foundation of any relationship is spirituality. It's not money. It's not good looks. It's not even his family background. The number one characteristic you look for in a man is his level of spirituality. This is not to say that you all cannot grow together if you are on one level and he is on another. It does not make you better than him if you happen to know more scriptures or clock longer hours in prayer, the point of the matter is, he is humble and willing to submit to the will of The Father or whomever his higher power may be. Yes, there are other factors that come into play right after spirituality, but I'm telling you that a man's level of spirituality or his potential to be at the appropriate level of understanding of how and when to pray, how and when to worship, and when and from whom to seek guidance beyond himself is paramount.

One of the problems with religion and the principle of spirituality is that there are so many versions and belief systems of what is right or wrong to worship. I'm not going to take time to explain that because who you decide to worship is up to you. My job, as your brother, is to encourage you to take a stance on being evenly yoked with your choice of man. Be patient with him as he matures, but true to yourself not to waiver in the expectation to choose a mate who desires to constantly move in a positive direction by maximizing spirituality in your relationship. Do not compromise on the principle of spirituality.

Empowerment Tools:

- Understand the importance of spirituality in your relationship
- Single Ladies, choose a man whose spiritual beliefs are congruent with yours
- Married Ladies, understand the struggles that your man may have regarding his spiritual growth
- Men should be able to experience God when he experiences the love of a woman

Go to work on yourself as hard as you can.

Chapter 14

What To Do While You Wait

May I ask you a few questions? Who are you? Where do you want to be mentally, physically, emotionally, and financially before marriage? Are you healed from past heartbreaks? What do you want to do with your life? Do you know who you are? Will a man be an enhancement to your life or a distraction? Are you equipped for marriage? What things should you be working on while you wait for your mate? These are just a few of the questions you should be asking yourself and finding the answers to these questions should be your number one priority.

When I think of a chapter that I want you to read at least two to three times, this is the chapter. This topic is for the women who may not have had a father figure in their lives to guide them as well as for the women who may be struggling with being at an age where you may be asking yourself, "Why can't I find a man?" The bigger, better question should be, **"What should I be doing while I am waiting?** I will address that question throughout the chapter, but first I need something from you. I need you to open your mind and receive the feedback you are reading. Act as if all that you have known thus far on how to meet and get involved in a successful relationship may have been wrong. Let this chapter speak to you and guide you to a better place. Now, there are several ways to answer this question but allow Harold Brinkley to give you the quick answer. He says, "*She should be living her life for herself, Number 1, and finding out what makes her happy. Number 2, she should be in the gym working out. Number 3...continually figuring out a way to make herself a better person every day.*

Harold gave us a quick answer to the question but women will hear pieces of that answer and not realize that there is a disconnection between information and implementation. Some women even talk about praying to God for a husband but very rarely are women taught how to properly pray and prepare for the marriage she desires. Let's travel a bit deeper and see what specific things you should be engaging in to help you properly prepare while you wait.

Chris Jackson: *Faith without works is dead. So unless you're constantly working on yourself, then the faith is going to be dead. It's a constant evolution of who you are and who you're going to attract...fall in love with your life. Fall in love with you. The reason why those things are key is because in a relationship or in a marriage you can get worn down and a marriage can bring you so much joy, but it can also bring you so much pain. If you are not of sound mind and body and loving yourself and your life, then you will allow a relationship to consume you and possibly tear you apart.*

James Foulke: *Number one, I would say that she needs to love herself. She needs to continue to gather her accolades and her own successes because life is hard when you don't have any money... and just continue to work on you... If you don't have yourself together, I don't think that you can expect somebody else to be a part of what you have going on... so you need to be the best person that you can be and love yourself. I will tell my daughters that you need to be the best you that you can be before you can expect somebody else to be joined up with you.*

Chancey King: *The number one thing they should be doing is building themselves up so that they can survive a life of their own... meaning that if a man never came into their life, they still need to know how to live and survive and not be depressed and not have a lack of self-esteem. She now knows that she doesn't have to chase anybody down because he is going to find her... because she is more of that hidden treasure, not him. He's the one that has the search for her. So that is one of the most important things is to immerse herself into becoming better at who she is. For example, I have a friend who is going through a divorce. She is about to let her husband know that she is leaving. Her mom thinks that she has someone else in her life. So she texted her mom the other day and she said "you know what? You are right. I have met someone else that's in my life, and I want to introduce you to that person. I hope that you will receive them with open arms." And she put the name of that person in her text and said "this is the person"... the name of that person was her own name. She put her own name in the text. She was letting her mother know, 'I have met myself. I'm falling in love with myself, and that's something I never did before I got married... and that's the person that I have met, and that's who I'm in love with..." and she never did that before marriage... now she's at the point of trying to change that and do what should have been done at first.*

For those of you who have been praying night after night about God sending you a man, why would He do that if you haven't begun to work on your purpose? You have a gift inside you that needs to be shared with the world. A gift that will not only enhance your life, but help make someone else better as well. Please stop putting the cart before the horse by trying to fulfill your relationship status when you haven't even put the due diligence in on your reason for existing on this Earth. You are NOT just here to have a few babies for a man. You are NOT here just to be in a relationship and have your husband care for you for the rest of your life. Get rid of those thoughts. Could that thought process be the reason why you have had so many struggles in relationships thus far? Some women should be happy that their prayers have not been answered because had your prayers been answered, you could have jacked up the relationship or influenced a good man to take a turn for the worse. Not because you are a bad person but because you may not have been as ready as you perceived yourself to be. When you pray, ask God to make you the wife He wants you to be and not one that society says you should be.

There is so much more to preparing for marriage than the average person realizes. What books are you reading? What personal development seminars are you attending? Sex tricks, cooking abilities, and good looks will never be good enough to make a man stay with you if your mental capacity is not ready to receive the blessings that a marriage can add to your life. Go to work on yourself as hard as you can. Meanwhile, The Creator will prepare someone just for you. As a matter of fact, your future husband is actually going through his own respective journey and preparing to meet you. Instead of begging God to send a man, I encourage you to prepare your mind, body, and soul for his arrival. There will be many counterfeit men that may come your way that you may think is your "soulmate" but the one who is destined to be your "right choice" will not come, if you do not personally develop yourself before he arrives.

One of the distractions that exists in society is that women are told to focus on utilizing the internet or be in certain places and that is what will help them meet quality men. That is the wrong idea and women should reject these alternative facts of how to find a man. Truth is, if you go to work on yourself and focus on your personal development, you won't have time to use tricks to get a man. You will "catch" a man but is this the person you want to spend the rest of your life with? There is nothing wrong with internet dating or attending mixers tailored to singles but it's all about your motives. I encourage you to relax and spend more time enjoying life by traveling and doing other things that you enjoy. Take the pressure off of yourself to perform or audition to be a wife. Your job is to be the mate you'd want to marry.

Here's more advice from our panel.

Porter Bingham: *Just don't worry about it. Just go on about life. You have a lot of things that you have to accomplish and you have a lot of things in life that you're trying to accomplish in the process of life. When God is ready to put the right person in place for you, then it will happen... and I'm not saying don't date people... get to know a lot of people and the choice will be obvious...*

Barry Case: *First thing would be to listen and obey. Prayer is a conversation between you and God. If I'm communicating with God, there's going to be a response. It's going to be some instruction. So you need to be sensitive to His voice and implement those instructions. You don't just pray aimlessly and ask for advice… no... you're praying for direction and you need to take that direction. The second thing, DO YOU.... meaning run your race. I almost want to say, "Let the game come to you" because sometimes when you're trying to make things happen you actually do more damage. Sometimes you have to let the game come to you… relax…. don't say, "Hey, I'm in my thirties or in my forties and I ain't got no man," and then you start to looking thirsty and you start entertaining dudes that you shouldn't… and now you slept with this guy and you're going to mess up the moment... if you were in your space doing your thing, he's going to find you. You have to trust and believe if you're running your race and doing you, than the dude is going to find you… and the good thing about it is that if you're doing you, the dude is going to find you in your space and it's authentic... but if you go putting yourself in a situation "hey, I'm going to go to a club because no dudes are coming to the library:, …now you in the club, a dude finds you, and that's not even who you are... and women say things like, "I need to put myself out there so I can be seen"... Don't be in any spaces that are not authentic to you because if you do, then you're not going to find the right company. If you're in somewhere or someplace that you have no business being, you're actually setting the guy up because he's thinking that you might be a certain type of person and you're really not…. you're just there because you're thirsty for a man.*

The constant theme that the men shared with you was just relax and don't worry about when your husband is coming. The right man will show up at the right time. Please stop saying, "I need to find a man." You don't need to find a man because it doesn't work like that. The man will find you the moment you are content with who you are and where you are in life.

Please stop saying, "Where are all the good men?" or "I need to put myself out there so I can catch a man." You cannot "catch" your man. You're not a glove... better yet you're not even a "good catch". There is no such thing as a "good catch". The word "catch" implies that you need to trap a man and that's not something you really are looking to do. You don't have a man because you are not ready for the man your prayers have asked for. Period. If you want what your prayers have asked for, become who you should be. Go work on yourself.

Here are final remarks from Zachary and Rodney:

Zachary King: *I would ask her to ask the Creator to have her get as connected as possible to what her purpose is right now...know from the Creator what your purpose is and serving the Creator... and you want to be like that when you're married… and when you're in good times and bad, you always want to have that peace…. if you're going to God and you're asking him for a spouse, but then when you get with that spouse, you get less as far as religion is concerned, then that's not good. You might as well stay single. Get connected to what your purpose is and start taking action so the Creator could start exposing it to you...and if you discard your values to acquire a spouse, you can actually get less and that could really impact your life long-term.*

Rodney Lawson: *She needs to live her life and she needs to date and don't just be secluded.. she needs to meet people so she can understand the differences that exist in people... a lot of times people don't know what they want and might be praying for something and it might come but it's not in the form that you thought it was going to be in ... I would definitely say she needs to build up on her foundation and that's financially, spiritually, educationally, so you're continuing to grow. Last but not least she needs to know what his values are and let me speak on that for a second so you can understand... keep in mind I know you might be thinking, "how can she understand his values before he comes?" ...but let me take this back to something I said earlier that I have to have loyalty...affection...transparency and strength in a woman... so what I'm saying is she needs to understand what she's looking for from the value perspective...she needs to have a clear-cut of what is going to fulfill her and if she does not understand that, she's not going to find it and she's just going to pick somebody off of infatuation...but if she knows what she's looking for from a values perspective, then as she meets these men, she will be more equipped to determine if this is the one for me or not.*

What are your core values? What are your deal breakers? An important part of your preparation process is being clear on what your values are and how they will impact your mate. The definition of the word "values" is the regard that something is held to deserve; the importance, worth, or usefulness of something; a person's principles or standards of behavior; one's judgment of what is important in life. In other words, take a few moments to write down what your values are. This is not to be confused with "the checklist" or preferences but values are those non-negotiable pillars that must be a part of your life.

While you are working on becoming what The Creator placed you on this earth to be, I encourage you to focus on a complete understanding of the principles, standards, and behavior of what you want your man to have and be. What is acceptable and unacceptable? The 80-20 Rule we spoke of earlier will not apply here. These are non-negotiable must haves. These are the basic building blocks you will want your daughter to focus on should she choose a mate one day.

Empowerment Tools:

- Focus on self-improvement and becoming what your Creator put you here for
- Prepare your mind, body and spirit to be the wife you were created to be
- Don't listen to the clichés from society about how to "catch" a man. Be patient and let the man find you
- Know what values you would like to see within your husband before you meet him
- Relax and enjoy your life while you wait.

...women need to understand that our needs change and we need you to be sensitive to our changes even if we are unable to articulate that a change has been made.

Chapter 15

Relationship Maintenance

In the words of Comedian Chris Rock, Men only need three things from their wives, "Feed me, f*** me, and shut the f*** up." I remember laughing hysterically when I heard him say this and at the time I was about four years away from being married and not in the mindset of settling down. After being married for some time, I started to think what he said may have more validity than what I may have realized. I raised a question to the men to see what their thoughts were regarding a woman's role in maintaining her relationship. ***As it relates to the role of a married woman, the maintenance of her man can be simple; respect him, cheer him on, sex him regularly, and feed him. Do you feel that men are this simple?***

Although I believe that men are simple to please, there are other factors that are just as important that need to be accomplished by a wife. Later in this chapter, we will discuss some of those additions, but for now, let's look at the responses of some of the married men on our panel whose tenure in marriage ranges from 10 to 30+ years.

Porter Bingham: *...Chris Rock was a comedian and his job was to sell albums. I do understand what he was saying because of the framework of the relationship with a man... you can take a bird's eye view and say generally what are guys looking for = the 3Fs, and don't nag me is really what he's saying for the last one... I think that's probably true...if you can have those three things, then a woman can generally get anything she wants.*

James Foulke: *Yes. We are cave beasts and we don't need very much. That's all I need. The world is alright to me after that.*

Sam Smith: *Yes, I think I'm the same minus the "feed me" part. I'm pretty easy and I'm just self-sufficient when it comes to food...I can deal with a bowl of cereal and it's no big deal.*

John Telley Gilliard: *If you have a woman that makes you feel good and tells you, "Baby, I value you, I appreciate you," and puts it on you and feeds you.... Yeah, that's all you ever truly need as a man. I'm very self-sufficient and I can do everything I need to do... But sex, I can't do by myself. I can do laundry. I can cook. I can have a job. I can keep a clean house. I can do whatever I need to do...but sex I can't do by myself.*

Donald Bell: *To a certain degree I really do... maybe not in that order but our needs are pretty basic. Your appreciation and respect go hand-in-hand and they are huge because we suffer so much disrespect outside in Corporate America and in society...so the respect and the appreciation are the cheerleading... the "ra ra" support... the "I have a dream" and you supporting me in the dream is paramount in a relationship... having a good, cooked meal, that's huge. Having outstanding sex is huge... outside of those, with the plus and minus factor of one or two, that's about it for men.*

Omar Finley: *Yes... I can't even lie about that one.... some people try to make things too complicated. Your man will literally die for you if he gets those things. He'll be like, "That's my woman... she's my ride or die chick!!!"*

Now, Ladies as you are reviewing these answers, I want you to know that I do believe that men are this simple. Consider your husband like another child in your home. Not in a disrespectful way but in his need for love, respect, care, support, and being nurtured by you. Although he may go out every day and fight for what your home needs when he comes home, his needs are simple.

Every day, he goes out and tries to play the game to win and you are his cheerleader. You are who he looks to for validation of how he is playing the game. But just like with any player in a game, there are basic needs that he has in order to go play the game. If I played a sport, there are certain foods, exercises, and specific coaching I would need to be successful when it's time to play. I want you to look at these basic factors in that same manner. Although each game may be different and certain factors can come into play that may demand your attention, I want you to focus on these factors as the basics. If you cover the basics, it will allow your man to always be the starter on your family's team. It will allow him to lace up every day and say, "I'm ready to play." And to highlight Omar's point, if you have these basics covered "your man will literally die for you."

I would be remiss if I failed to share the thoughts of some of the married men who feel slightly different.

Barry Case: *No, I don't think that it's that simple. I think that everybody is complex and different situations are going to bring about different needs and different emotions. I'm going to be transparent. A couple of weeks ago my wife was like "yeah, why you not trying to get at a sista?" ... and I'm like "you know what baby, I'm so focused on so many other things and not that that's right, but my libido is not like it was before in thinking about, "sex, sex, sex"... I'm thinking about, "I gotta finish up this master's degree, I got to pay this mortgage", and my mind has been bothered by so many other things... "I got to take care of my family, I got to take care of responsibilities."... so I'm now at place I have evolved, whereas, sex is just not the only thing that satisfies me... now, I'm like "Yo, let me make sure my kids are taken care of..."*

To Barry's point, he shifts from some of the basics to a deeper perspective. The statement, "now I'm at the place."... is key because he shares with us that he used to be "simple", but later on he shifted into a broader perspective of his role as a husband and father. As a wife, I encourage you to be ready to make the adjustment as your husband adjusts. At one point, he may have needed sex five times per week, a hot meal promptly at 6:00 pm each night, and 30 minutes of quiet time when he walked in the door from work. Your role is to do your part to help maintain the relationship by staying on top of his needs as he evolves as a man. Let's review Rodney and Chris' perspective regarding the simplicity of a man's needs.

Rodney Lawson: *No, I do not. It is much more complex than that but the problem is that a lot more men don't communicate, which is why I'm on a mission to not only help myself from being broken but also work with other men who are broken but don't realize that they are broken. The problem is that men are taught to keep their emotions inside since they were a child and the problem is we're not taught to have an outlet. That's why we can come across so angry at times because when those things start to overload, we start to react in ways that should not be a part of our character.*

Chris Jackson: *I wish more people understood Maslow's hierarchy of needs and we would never have to have this conversation. We understand that these are really the basic needs. Those first three that are...sex...food and... feelings of appreciation. If you tap into those first three levels of a man, then you still have so much more that you need to learn and understand about a man. When you get to the level of understanding how a man thinks and when you understand how a man loves a woman, and...once he loves her, he will run through brick walls to take care of her and to give her everything that she needs and he will stop at nothing to make sure that woman does not need for anything... But what happens many times in our relationships, we stop short of the first three levels.*

Based on the feedback from Rodney and Chris, it may sound as if the surface level of our basic needs are understood, but there may be some additional factors that women may need to consider when caring for their man. My subsequent question to the panel of men was, ***"After reviewing these 3 basic factors, give one thing you would add to this theory."***

James Foulke: **pause*... I mean there's really nothing else.... but the only thing that I can think of is...make just as much money if not more than me... that's really all I can think of...*

Sam Smith: *Give me feedback because life is not perfect and I'm not perfect. How can I show up differently? What adjustments can I make as a man so I can make life better for our relationship, our goals, etc?*

Omar Finley: *Listen to him. Because people change over time... as you get older, people change and if we don't evolve together, we'll grow apart.*

Rafiq Shakur: *I believe they are going to have to laugh together. The litmus test of any relationship is how often they laugh. You can go out in public and look around and if you watch a couple that's laughing, I promise that translates to every other part of their relationship... so yes they're going to have to laugh together. It sounds simple and might sound stupid, but if there's no laughter, if there is no humor in the relationship, it's on its way out.*

John Telley Gilliard: *Be consistent. You can't do all that stuff one day and then cut the next couple of weeks. That's what they expect from us, being consistent.... So you need to be consistent as well.*

Porter Bingham: *The one thing I would add to that theory would be to be a helpmate in the mature sense of the term. I don't mean washing dishes and clothes, but providing an environment for him to thrive in... and if you have that, then that's all that you can ask for... When I say providing an environment to thrive in, I mean taking a modest interest in what her mate does... Understanding the day to day stresses that he goes through and making sure that when he crosses that threshold of his home, at least helping those things to be eliminated... and the man can be taken into a "spa type" place...an environment where he can relax, rejuvenate, have refuge, and get ready to go back out and slay the dragons again the next day.*

Outside of the basics of respecting him, cheering him on, sexing him regularly, and feeding him, there are many other factors to consider. Wives, I encourage you to focus on the basics but also pay attention to the other factors that your husband may need as he evolves as a man.

Single Ladies, be prepared to walk into your marriage ready to be an expert in the basics for your man. As time goes on and he opens up more of his other layers, you will see what other factors will present themselves as he evolves and matures in the relationship.

We understand that maintaining the relationship is not solely the woman's job but it is a collaborative effort from both parties, however, as we discuss marriage maintenance and how a man thinks, women need to understand that our needs change and we need you to be sensitive to our changes even if we are unable to articulate that a change has been made. We are not expecting you to be mind readers but we are asking you to pay attention and ask questions instead of ignoring us, taking our change personal and nagging about our change. As you take the time to understand how your man functions day after day and year after year, the two of you will evolve, grow, and thrive as a successfully married couple. Be mindful that what was important at year one may not be the same at year twenty-one. The point is to be prepared to shift. Maintenance is all about knowing when to make an adjustment in order to maintain a thriving, lasting relationship.

Empowerment Tools:

- Embrace the basics of respecting him, cheering him on, sexing him, and feeding him
- Consider other factors of:
  - evolving as a helpmate
  - actively listening to him
  - laughing with him
  - sharing useful feedback
  - help him make money
- Pay attention as he evolves as a man in order to maintain a lasting relationship

Conclusion

A couple of years ago, every Wednesday one of my fraternity brothers posted something positive about his wife on social media. He started calling the posts, "#wifeywednesday". Shortly after that, I began to post pictures and a little verbiage celebrating my wife in some form as well. Once I received the revelation about this manual I thought using social media would be a great platform to help women become somebody else's "#wifeywednesday". Periodically, I'd post quotes on my social media pertaining to this manual. Many of the quotes came from either the gentlemen that I'd interviewed or my personal thoughts that you've read throughout the manual. One of the things I'd noticed is that every time I'd make a post, there were a few women who would take offense or somehow receive the post in a negative manner. Many would even deviate from the overall intent of the post often turning it into a discussion of "double standards" and other controversial issues. Keep in mind that the posts were not derogatory, but were established to help women get closer to either being a wife or understanding their husband or just men in general. But as with most opportunities in life, you will always have individuals who resist the change that is necessary to become better. So knowing that this is a part of the human psyche, I never took offense to the opposition to the posts I'd put up. The reason that some women opposed the posts I'd made was that, unfortunately, the culture that has been created in our society is that men need to understand women more than women need to understand men. If you look at the songs, the movies, and the TV shows, the majority of all of these mediums are talking about how much more men need to do, and how much more men need to be better, and how much more men need to understand the needs of a woman. And even the information that sparingly does come out about women understanding men, the direction is more of women becoming *like* men instead of women being the woman she was designed to be. Men and women need to take the time to understand each other. Understanding the male and female species respectively is not a one-sided discussion and that was the purpose of this manual. Whether or not you agree with all of the points we've discussed does not matter. You can take the information you have received in this manual, apply it to your relationship, and the worst thing that will happen is that your relationship will become stronger as well as you becoming a better person

Women are the main coaches in the relationship. Women are smarter and have the innate ability to create the proper culture to allow the relationship to flourish. The man is the MVP or All-Star player of the team. The problem has been instead of the coach maximizing the player, understanding the player, and winning the game, the coaches have been trying to become the player and that's why on average the game keeps being lost. You now have the tools to win more games should you choose to accept the mission of understanding a man.

If we are going to build stronger communities, save and reform the traditional family, we have to start with the foundation of the woman and empower her with the tools to build and enhance lasting relationships alongside her man. The purpose of this manual was not to give women the weapons to win the war, it was to give you tools to win more battles against the evil forces attempting to keep you from having a successful, lasting relationship. And let me be clear by saying that men are not your enemy, Ladies. You need us just as much as we need you. The enemy is within our own minds which have been fueled by an ignorant society and culture that you should intentionally resist. The lack of understanding of the male thought process has assisted in the demise of many dating relationships and marriages but now you are more equipped to understand how to move past those battles of confusion and misunderstanding.

My challenge to you from here is to share this manual and the tools you've learned with your daughters, sisters, cousins, friends, co-workers or maybe even your mother. I also encourage you to share it with your sons and other members of the male species to reinforce what was shared within this manual. Share with your children the mistakes you've made and how the application of the information you have received in this manual has been helpful to you. Thank you in advance for sharing this ground-breaking information with those in your sphere of influence and helping to strengthen our communities, our families, and our world.

About the Author

Elam B. King, a Hackensack, NJ native is a profound Author, exhilarating Speaker, and provocative Thought Leader. After receiving a Bachelor of Science in Marketing from Hampton University, he went on to receive an MBA in Project Management and an MBA in Marketing from American Intercontinental University. He is the Vice President of a successful Advertising, Sales, Branding, and Mobile Application development firm and resides in Lithonia, Georgia. Elam is a proud husband and father of a blended family of 6.

Made in the USA
Columbia, SC
06 March 2018